THE CHURCH AND CREATION

THE CHURCH AND CREATION

TRANSLATED FROM THE SPANISH OF

LUIS COLOMER, O.F.M.

By

PALMER L. ROCKEY, Ph.D.

1956

ST. ANTHONY GUILD PRESS
PATERSON, NEW JERSEY

Nihil obstat:

BEDE BABO, O. S. B.,

Censor librorum.

Imprimatur:

† JAMES A. McNULTY,

Bishop of Paterson.

July 6, 1956.

PRINTED IN THE UNITED STATES OF AMERICA

FOREWORD

The very fact that a book is offered in translation is usually an indication that the original work is important. While it is true that worthless and even harmful books have boasted of wide circulation and have appeared in many languages, it is also true, and happily so, that good books, too, are made available to a wider circle of readers by means of translation.

THE CHURCH AND CREATION, as it appears in its English dress, is the second part of a work in Spanish by Fray Luis Colomer: LA IGLESIA CATOLICA. Palmer L. Rockey has previously translated the first part of that work under the title THE CATHOLIC CHURCH: THE MYSTICAL BODY OF CHRIST, and though the two parts belong together and give the reader a complete picture of that masterpiece of creation which is the Catholic Church, these separately published volumes can well be read apart from each other. It is to be hoped, however, and to be expected, that those who have read the one will be eager to go on to the other.

Perhaps the first point I should make in this brief introduction to Dr. Rockey's translation is to stress the fact that he has succeeded in putting into idiomatic, readable and even rhythmic English the sublimity of thought, clarity of presentation and frequently poetic language of the original. Even those who may have read this work in Spanish will have to admit that nothing of its original thought has been lost in the new dress, and I dare say that those who read only the translation will find the style free and easy throughout.

In referring to the contents of this masterly presentation of Christian theology on the relationship of the Church to the visible and invisible world, it should be noted that there is evidence here of a truly catholic — in the sense of *universal* — society, one that touches and transforms even material things in a manner that makes them serve the high purpose of religion. As Christ in the institution of the Sacraments made use of such common things as water and oil to signify, together with signs and words, a supernatural effect, thus also this book demonstrates with telling, irrefutable logic the power and authority of the Church to institute various rites and ceremonies whereby public worship as well as the private practice of religion is rendered noble, artistic, and attractive to man's nature.

Read further and learn how and why the high destiny and the real happiness of man are so intimately and so inevitably associated with Mother Church. Go on to the third chapter of the book and allow the author to show you the great importance of the first and smallest of societies, the family, and note how the Church with her divinely delegated authority watches over parents and children in the sanctuary of the home, how she protects that home with the mantle of tender motherhood and sublimates the natural ties of flesh and blood in a blessedness that is real even in this life, and permanent, reaching from the cradle to the grave and even beyond it.

The chapter entitled "The Church and the State" is one that should be read carefully and, I might add, prayerfully. In an age when totalitarianism in its most vicious form is threatening to engulf all the world, when it is being more widely realized that the one, holy, catholic and Apostolic Church is the last and only effective bulwark against the enslavement of all peoples of the world, it should be of interest not only to Catholics but to all lovers of political freedom to study the relationship of Christ and His Church to the

State. Fray Luis Colomer has handled this subject thoroughly
and tactfully, but also courageously, drawing his conclusions
with inevitable logic from Christ's own teaching and from a
convincing Scriptural background. The way to read this chapter is to keep your mind on past and current history and to
note that in every State where the influence and rights of
Mother Church were not or are not recognized, there the
rights of citizens also gradually disappear and even vanish.

Part II of this book is without doubt the most sublime of
the two divisions that make up the entire work. This, not
only because of the subject matter, which is by its very nature
far above that treated in the first four chapters and which
rises in dignity from chapter to chapter — the treatment by the
author also reaches new heights in sublimity of thought and
expression. While reading the first four chapters of this book,
I found myself wondering what a reader without the true
faith would make of them, whether he would follow through
and read to the end what the author has written on the Church,
her relation to man, the family, and the State. If such a reader
is intelligent enough and open-minded enough to go on, I
doubt not that those first four chapters would urge him to
more enlightened and reverent thinking on the important and
practical subjects therein treated; the man of faith would
never challenge the author, and if previously not too well
instructed, would learn much.

As for the second part of THE CHURCH AND CREATION,
however — while I was reading these four chapters, my soul
was fairly lifted up in a new appreciation of the sublimest
teaching directed by the voice of God to the listening heart
of man. Within me I felt the keen desire and expressed the
fervent hope that many, many readers would allow themselves to read on and on to the very end. They will enter

beyond the realm of human knowledge and rise to a participation in the divine.

Here is really much more than a glimpse of the invisible world; here, resting on God's word and the Sacred Scriptures, which are also His work — here, under the guidance of the Church and a capable theologian of that Church, you will consort more intimately with creatures a little above man, but not unconcerned about him; in fact you will find that some of these angels, under God's plan, have been created especially for the benefit of man, one for you individually, one whom even we of the faith too often forget and fail to appreciate.

And in these most modern times, when the Mother of Christ, the Mother of God, Mary, the Virgin-mother of Nazareth, is revealing herself more frequently and more intimately as also the Mother of the Church, the Mother of all men — if you are but slightly interested in Our Lady of Guadalupe, Our Lady of Lourdes, Our Lady of Fatima and now Our Lady of Heede, read the sixth chapter of this book and you will understand better why Mary, Christ's mother, is also the mother of the Church and is busy every day with Christ and with the Church in watching over all of us.

God's master plan in creation, His masterpiece, is Christ. Let the master theologian in this book tell you more about this plan and how it is still working, how you, too, small and insignificant in yourself, are also a part of that plan. And, as you reach the final chapter in this book, as you read of the Church and the Blessed Trinity, you will know so much more of God's life and your own life, you will know and be thrilled at the thought and also — pray God — you will rejoice in the faith and conviction that even you, however miserable a creature you may at times feel yourself to be, are destined to share not only the life of God but His glory as well. Fray Luis

Colomer and Dr. Rockey, his translator, are at your service. Walk with them a while and listen to their story of THE CHURCH AND CREATION.

VERY REVEREND AUGUSTINE HOBRECHT, O. F. M.

Province of Santa Barbara

CONTENTS

Part I

THE CHURCH'S RELATIONSHIP
WITH THE VISIBLE WORLD

Part I

CHAPTER I

THE CHURCH AND THE LOWER CREATURES

BECAUSE of His eminent dignity and His universal religious ministry, Jesus Christ has a relationship with everything that exists. So, too, the Church — because of what she is and what she does — likewise has a relationship with the whole universe; nothing is exempt from contact with her. The sacred bonds that exist between the lower creatures and the Church are what we are going to consider in this chapter.

I

The Church, a visible and supernatural society of men who live in time, necessarily needs material goods for the exercise of her vital functions and for the fulfillment of her mission. Although the deep principle of her life and her eternal destiny are very spiritual, she is subject to material needs with regard to her visible social body — necessities which cannot be satisfied without the use of suitable material goods. It is necessary that such goods, of limited usefulness, should be appropriated to the Church and remain her own by reason of firm and legitimate possession and, therefore, in virtue of a rigorous right to property on the part of the Church. The Church needs these material goods for the discharge of her sacred ministry, for the support of her priests, and for the inexhaustible and active exercise of her charity among men. Added to the reasons which every physical and moral person has for legitimately possessing material goods to the exclusion of other joint owners, the Church has the sacred one of the holiness of her ends.

In fact, the inevitable material and spiritual necessities of human life, both individual and collective, and the natural limitation of useful material goods, are the deep and permanent basis for their possession by him who legitimately makes them his own. If these goods were as abundant as air, there would be no reason to appropriate them in order to use them for immediate personal gain. And if they were as inappropriable as air or solar radiations, it would be useless to try to gather them as we do wheat or money. But they are neither all inappropriable, nor do they all possess inexhaustible fecundity such as would satisfy the universal need without effort on the part of anyone. Herein lies the invariable and pressing need for appropriating them in some way to a person or society which may develop them in such a way as to make them more productive and fitted to the needs of life. Hence arises the right of this person or society over them to the exclusion of the simultaneous right of others. In this way monopoly over things by one with detriment to another is avoided. Rather, the productivity of natural things multiplies for the benefit of many. A field which is well cultivated with plants for the sustenance of life, offers man what without human labor it would not give. He who possesses and invests in it cultivates it with the hope of obtaining a reasonable profit. Thus the produce of the well-cultivated field is beneficial not only to the one who possesses and cultivates it, but also to those who, in exchange for other things, acquire the fruits of this private property. With private property there is stimulus for work and progress, economic independence for him who owns a sufficiency, as well as an abundance, the use of which helps many others besides the owner of the field in question. And so it is in general with regard to all possessions when they are maintained within the legitimate limits which reason and common sense, justice, and equity demand. Once these limits and norms are overthrown, private property is converted into an instrument of tyranny and a source of disorder, just as overeating may be the source of malfunctioning organs and habitually excessive satisfaction of any natural need can cause damage and must be avoided.

Private property and common property have their roots in nature and are a natural right just as the right to preserve one's life or the right of man to human dignity or to the legitimate liberty of all the children of Adam.

During the course of her existence in this world, the Church is equally subject to needs which normally can be completely satisfied only by the certain possession of material goods. Whatever through natural right cannot be denied either to man or to the family or to a legitimate society cannot be denied to the Church. The Church exists by the will of Jesus Christ, Lord and King of creation; she also exists for the loftiest end possible in this life, one which all men without exception are called upon to seek and obliged to seek. The vital and permanent needs of the Church, arising from the duty of fulfilling her sublime end within the circumstances of the present life, are the firm and ineradicable root of her right to possess material goods, just as her sovereignty gives her the claim to employ them for her own use without subjection to outside powers.

Divine worship and the exercise of the vital functions in the interest of souls require churches. The upkeep of these demands economic means without which churches could not subsist and the vital functions of the Church could not be discharged. These functions are not performed without sacred ministers to discharge them; these, because of their sacred character and ministry, are set apart from the world and withdrawn from profane affairs. Hence it is necessary that the Church should possess goods for the proper sustenance of her priests, and that the latter should never be in such straits that they have to engage in affairs that are incompatible with their sacred ministry, in order to attend to the urgent and tyrannical necessities of life. Finally, it is indispensable for the Church who, in her tireless charity towards all the physically and spiritually needy, so solicitously attends to the many miseries in the world — it is indispensable for her to possess the means for filling such great needs, which no human power has attempted to fill as has the Holy Spouse of Jesus Christ. From her first days in Jerusalem, the Church has looked after orphans and widows, the infirm and the destitute. In a word, wherever this blessed society of Christ-loving souls has been present and in action, it has cared for all the afflicted and needy members of the human society.

A society which has such a lofty foundation as does the Church, and which exists for such elevated ends and ministries, cannot lack the elementary and natural right which is possessed by an industrial or commercial society directed towards the individual wealth of its members through the exploitation of goods of more or less extensive usefulness. Therefore the Church has the legitimate right to possess as much as she needs for the discharge of her ministry and the sustenance of her life on earth.

Yet there is more to be noted. Although the right to property is a natural one, since it is rooted in the present universal conditions of man's life, neither the individual nor imperfect and incomplete societies can extend this right without bounds, to the detriment of others. Proper order with regard to this right demands a central authority. To this authority must be entrusted the common good of all, so that it becomes a guarantee of all rights and of the law, seeing to it that each member fulfills his duties. Thus this authority curbs the unrestrained desires of individuals or the improper administration of goods which, though they constitute private property, do not cease to be of common utility and thus must be employed for the prosperity and profit of all. It is here that the State, which is the supreme authority in human affairs, may have the right to put prudent limitations on the natural right of its subjects. It can do this so that the plan of Divine Providence for the common good may not be exchanged for social upheaval and for oppression and tyranny on the part of a few over the multitudes enslaved by hunger. From the very same end of safeguarding the social order, of procuring the common good, and protecting the rights of all, springs the State's right to regulate the right to property prudently and to intervene in the exercise of such a right for its subjects when necessity demands.

The Church is not subject to the authority of the State in this matter. The State has no legitimate right to intervene in the administration of the Church's goods. The reason for this is apparent. A State has no right to govern another equally legitimate and sovereign State. One State as such is not subject to another, nor to any foreign earthly authority. Therefore no State has the right to impose restrictions on another State's legitimate discharge of its functions, nor to infringe upon its natural right to ownership, as long as it does not invade the legitimate domain of another State. To intervene in another State's internal affairs, to dispossess it or its subjects of their legitimate rights within their own territory, would be intolerable intrusion and manifest tyranny. Such an action would in fact annul the independence and sovereignty of the violated State. Hence the Church, which is a perfect society, of itself fully capable of legitimately discharging its functions and of attaining its end — a society which springs immediately from God, who has not put it under any other power — cannot be supervised by any other State in the world. No State can interfere with the Church's right to possess and administer her own goods. Hence she may proceed in her affairs without intervention from foreign powers, which have no right to subject her to their will.

One may say that since the Church has no territory of her own and since she is present within the territory of other States, her goods fall under the supervision and rights of the latter wherever the proper use of the right of property by subjects of the State is concerned. It is true that the Church does not have territory of her own, as a State alongside others. Yet in what she possesses as a society she cannot acknowledge any sovereignty other than her own, under the penalty of losing it by subjecting herself to another's sovereignty. Her very fullness and perfection demand this independence. And States cannot help but recognize it once they understand her status as a universal and sovereign society. Only reasonably regulative agreements concerning her property rights within the territory of the State with which she deals, can be proper in this matter. The State in question cannot impose laws which overlook or scorn the Church's rights. To do so would be to tyrannize an international power which, though weak in arms, counts upon the divine assistance which ultimately causes oppressive States to pay dearly for their crimes against the Church.

There is another outstanding characteristic with regard to the right to property, namely, its sacred character. The Church is a supernatural society and a divine being existing for divine purposes. Property, required because of the necessities connected with her existence and the accomplishment of her ends, cannot but receive in the Church something of a sacred character, since it more or less directly concerns the service of God. Churches and sacred vessels, altars, images and vestments, whatever pertains to divine worship, are material goods dedicated directly to divine worship and hence all are blessed and certain ones consecrated. These goods must not be confused with those of a mercantile house or a privately owned home or industry. Since they are dedicated to God they are indeed sacred. Abuse of them is profanation; robbery, a sacrilege.

The material possessions which serve to sustain the sacred ministers of the Church, as well as those of her institutions of learning and charity, are not, of course, directly consecrated to divine service. Yet they are sacred because the Church possesses them and because of the definitive end for which they are destined: that is, the extension of the kingdom of God in souls. This end must not be confused with the end which natural societies have. Material possessions which are held by a subject such as the Church and directed towards an end such as the Church has, cannot be ranked with worldly goods. Such goods have in them the traces of something holy and sacred. Hence any outrage against them involves a special crime, one that concerns the abuse of God's gifts and natural goods. For this reason, the despotic interference of States with regard to the possessions of the Church, now through confiscation, now through the impeding of their free administration by those who legitimately possess them, and who hold dominion over these things as well as others which pertain to the social existence of the Church, is an intolerable abuse of force. It is a sacrilegious crime committed against the divine sovereignty of the holy Spouse of Jesus Christ. The Church has never rejected a reasonable agreement with the State. Rather, she has often condescended to renounce her own possessions for the benefit of the needy State or for the maintenance of peace. What she cannot tolerate without protesting is the non-recognition of her sovereignty and of the fullness of her right to possess and administer her own goods independently of any earthly authority.

Thus has been explained the most humble and visible relationship between the Church and material things. These are necessary to the Church, that she may achieve the purpose of her existence; she possesses them legitimately through acts of irreproachable accession; she administers them with the holy liberty which God gave her that she might exist and spread over the whole earth. But besides this juridical relation with certain things, the Church has higher and more extensive ones with all the rest of creation. This is true especially with regard to those things that form the world in which we live and with which our life is more directly concerned. We shall consider these relations in the following section.

II

We frequently see priests and bishops bless material things which are useful to men. Among these can be listed homes, automobiles, railroads, ships, and airplanes. To this list can be added those things which the churches use in their worship and those employed by the faithful for increasing devotion and piety. Are these blessings perhaps vain ceremonies? Are they perhaps a sterile expression of good desires on the part of the Church? No, such is not the case. Priests and the faithful sincerely believe in the spiritual efficacy of these blessings. The Church in her holy and deep sincerity would not permit them unless she was infallibly certain that these words and rites of blessing are not simply things thrown to the winds.

The blessing of material things by the Church concerns a vital truth and has a very deep meaning.

Two predominant ideas are to be noted in the formulas for blessings employed by the Church: (1) the drawing down of divine favor on the things blessed and on those who use them properly; (2) the exclusion of Satan's power from them. Sometimes these two ideas are joined in one formula.[1] At other times only one appears.[2] By reading the Roman Ritual attentively, we clearly see how the Church employs the efficacy of the blessing to ward off the enemy of mankind and to draw down God's gifts upon mankind. Granted the divine assistance to the Church's authority and the prudent way in which the latter proceeds in its teachings and practices, there is no doubt that the blessing of things is no vain ceremony but a sacred rite full of meaning, having a mysterious reality and operative efficacy when the proper conditions are present.

Certain it is that through sin man is subject to the harsh rule of the devil, even though he is free to resist the latter's evil suggestions. It is also certain that the lower creation has been vitiated and blemished by sin and put, in a certain sense, under the will of the spirit of evil, who uses it to tempt man. We cannot explain how this satanic dominion is effected, nor to what point the justice of God allows the enemy to use material things to assail us, or to what extent the enemy employs these things to carry out his perverse plans and evil assaults. Saint Paul tells us about our secret battle against principalities and powers on high.[3] Saint Anthony Abbot suffered frequent assaults from the devil, who took on frightening forms of animals and moved the elements, it seems, to threaten

---

[1]As in the case of the blessing of holy water and the blessing of animals.
[2]As in the blessing of a new house, fruits of the fields, etc.
[3]Cf. Eph. 6:12.

the saint. Saint Catherine of Siena saw infernal monsters who filled her room like a swarm of flies, flee in terror when she invoked the holy name of Jesus against them.[4] Reason illumined by faith knows that sin has delivered man over to the wild wrath of the devil. It also knows, however, that man is still free and that he still has the power of effecting his sanctification by co-operating with grace. Yet reason illumined by faith is not blind to the fact that the enemy tyrannizes material creatures which serve man in many ways in the sustenance and progress of the life of the individual and of society. Once the reality of diabolical infestation is admitted — that is, the devil's influence on material creatures — it is clear that the Church feels that she has the power and the right to repel the enemy and to cleanse the creatures she blesses of Satan's action and secret contact. The Church holds this, knowing she is vivified by the Spirit of Jesus, vitally united to her Divine Head, and in possession of the efficacious power of her Spouse for the salvation of souls. She could not treat otherwise things which she uses for divine service, for conveying her love and petitions to God, and for expressing her pure and ardent affection for her Spouse. She blesses all the objects destined for divine worship in order to cleanse them from the traces of sin with which human baseness has stamped them. She also blesses them in order to cleanse them of the impurities which the devil has secretly poured into them through his evil action and destructive power.

There is no reason why the purifying efficacy of the Church's blessing should be limited to objects destined for liturgical services or for the increase of piety, such as images, medals, scapulars, and cords. The Christian is a member of

---

4Jörgensen, *St. Catherine of Siena*, Book I, chapter vi.

Jesus Christ and the object of loving care and holy gifts on the part of the Mother of the children of God. Even those who are not Christians are called to this dignity. The Spouse of Jesus Christ cannot help but love them and seek them out with indefatigable zeal. Those who have been torn from the living being of the Church through heresy, schism, or apostasy are also drawn back to this divine society of souls by urgent appeals and fervent prayers. All of them need material things in order to live and to elevate their souls to God. Both groups are in incessant and active contact with the material things of nature. Can there be any doubt that the Church can heal nature of the infestation of the one who malevolently makes use of it for the ruin of souls? Or is there any reason to doubt that the Church's blessing can fall on a thousand things placed by Providence in the world for man's use, relieving them of a mysterious diabolical weight and of Satan's frightful action? Assuredly not. Therefore it is not strange that the Church blesses many things which are not to be used for divine worship but are to be employed by men for the ordinary affairs of life. Nor is it any wonder that the Church invokes the power of God in these cases to ward off the action of the enemy, who makes use of creatures for the perdition of the children of Adam. Our Lord's merits extend over the whole of creation like an inextinguishable halo of light. In like manner, the Spouse of Christ extends her hands, full of the merits of her Bridegroom, over this lower creation, in order to restore it and to heal it of a mysterious and obstinate diabolical infestation.

This is one of the beneficent effects wrought by the blessings of the Church. The other is the no less mysterious drawing down of divine benefits upon blessed objects and upon those who know how to use them reverently.

Diabolical action in the material world is an episode in the great drama of creation and a divine permission which fixes limits — in space, in time, and in manner — to the evil action of one who, in spite of his stubborn rebellion, cannot shake off the yoke of God's universal sovereignty. The divine action in creatures, on the contrary, is constant, profound, and without limits. It embraces all and sustains all with indefatigable power and omnipotent love. God is everywhere; He is in the innermost depths of beings, as an omniscient observer of what is there and of what happens, as a very active intelligent power that sustains and governs all and seeks the divine glory through the intelligent acts of the higher creatures united with Christ for the plenitude of their eternal destiny. Each creature is a note in the universal canticle of the glory of God, a profound vibration of a creative love which is manifested in every way as an inexhaustible source of blessings for the one whom God has wished to make to His image and likeness, as well as raise to the dignity of being His son and a brother of Jesus Christ. The Church has a deep and vital belief that God is present in all that exists. Furthermore, she knows that everything has been elevated and ennobled in Jesus Christ and that even the lower creation has been penetrated by the rays of supernatural dignity which pulsate as a glorious life in the children of God in heaven. The pure and glowing heart of Saint Francis of Assisi seemed to perceive the divine warmth of the invisible action of God in creatures. And as though he were their heart and tongue, he sang to God for them, as if they were his brothers. Thus he called the gleaming sun Brother, and the fresh and limpid water Sister. All the good these contain they incessantly receive from God, without interruption or pause in the loving and creative action. Is it strange that the Church should implore the Lord to give fruitfulness and efficacy to things as a help for human needs? Is it strange that to the natural virtue of creatures she adds free supernatural gifts which stimulate souls to love God?

The Church has a profound faith in the inexhaustible merits of her Bridegroom and a limitless confidence in the bounty of the heavenly Father. Better than any saint, and with more purity and certainty than all of them together, she is aware of this loving presence of God in creatures. In gathering to her motherly heart all the needs of her children, and in contemplating with the eyes of charity those among men called to the dignity of being her members — although now they are not such, or, having been such, have torn themselves away from her — could she fail to turn to Him who vivifies and sustains her with His omnipotent spirit and beseech Him to shower His favors on created things unknowingly hungry for divine life? This is what the Church does in blessings that implore the divine favor. God cannot reject the humble and confident prayer of the faithful Spouse of His Son made man. The Church's merits will not pass unnoticed in the divine presence, nor will her impetrative power ever fail or cease. Hence our Lord will infallibly attend to the desire of His Church and certainly sanctify and improve, with His invisible benediction, what she visibly blesses and sanctifies through the hands of her sacred ministers.

This blessing comes down upon and is extended to material creatures in an indefinite — or better, limitless — sphere. The power of the Church is not restricted in this regard. She blesses the land and water, the fields and woods, the air and sea. There is no material thing in the world to which she cannot extend her benediction, and which is not capable of receiving this divine touch that purifies and gives the increase. It would seem that the mysterious creative action of divine love which sustains all, effects more delicate and abundant effusions in things touched by the blessing of the Church. It is an outpouring of divine love on behalf of men; it is called forth by the intercession of the Church. And it comes through the magic thread of creatures who are blessed. Just as all things are subject to the glorious power of Jesus Christ, so they can be touched and improved by the blessing of the Spouse of Christ. The Church thus puts the devil to flight and draws divine favors upon all that she blesses and on behalf of those who reverently use these blessings.

This uplifting action of the Church upon material things does not concern the possession and use of them as necessities of life, but is a delicate spiritual action, an infusion into them by one who is full of divine life and who has the mission of spreading it to men's souls. It is a trace of the splendor of Jesus' curative power exercised in these created things through which His mission visibly proceeds among men; and it is the mystical prolongation of the Redeemer's life. We can thus see raised to God, through the medium of the Church, all these humble creations placed by divine bounty at the side of men that they might sustain them in their fatiguing journey through life and help them climb their eternal destiny on the steps of intelligence and love.

Yet the uplifting spiritual action of the Church upon material creation does not stop here. The Church uses many things in carrying out divine worship and thus makes them serve as instruments in the divine praise and in the sacrifice of adoration. The sweet-smelling incense burning before the altar, the lighted candles in the church, the oil that keeps alive the holy flame in sanctuary lamps, the flowers that beautify and fill the house of God with fragrance — whatever is used in divine worship, be it a work of nature or of art, is a sensible expression of the sentiments of the Spouse of Jesus Christ and of her regard for her Divine Bridegroom and all that concerns and belongs to Him. These are not only things that have been blessed by the Church and purified from all traces of sin and the infestation of Satan. They are also associated with a sacred function and are instruments of its expression in the Church. Such creation, then, becomes the vehicles of divine ideas and glows with the fire of sacred affections. Eyes brightened by the interior glow of a great idea or the fire of a powerful affection, cheeks flushed by the warmth of a deep emotion, are expressions of the life of the soul which is really manifested in these physical organs, mirrors of the interior spiritual life. Likewise, through the material things which the ministers of the Lord use for divine worship according to the norms of the Church, there also passes a mysterious flow of life whose salutary effects cannot be experimentally perceived by us. Yet they are no less real because of our incapacity to experience them. The idea in the mind pulsates in the audible sound of man's word as it intelligently brings the latter into the world. In like manner the soul of the Church breathes in the clanging of bells, in the spirals of burning incense, in the flames of candles, in the harmonies of the organ, in the beautifully shaped marble of our ancient cathedrals, and in the delicate filigree of sacred vessels. The Church associates all these things with her prayer and her religious actions, to serve as a transparent veil of her ideas and an eloquent expression of her love in her sure movement towards God.

But the Church's spiritualization of the material world penetrates even further than we have yet mentioned. By the institution of the sacraments, Jesus has raised humble matter to greater heights. He has made it a mysterious conductor of divine life. A copper wire stretched through the air from a source of electrical energy carries invisible power which may light lamps, move powerful machines, and be the source of many conveniences. In like manner, Jesus has made sacramental matter a mysterious wire conducting the divine life which vivifies the children of God. The Church sings inspired words concerning this mysterious action of the Holy Spirit in baptismal water, in the holy chrism with which the Church consecrates the priests of the Lord and anoints the sick in danger of death. And in the sacred hands of her priests, the Church reverently takes bread and wine, which, through the omnipotent words of the consecration, are changed into the body and blood of Jesus Christ, though the appearances of bread and wine are preserved. It seems that here matter attains the depths of the divine life and that it is the omnipotent hand of Jesus which effects well-being or life in whatever it touches. Hence it is not strange that the Church, in singing the divine praises, should associate the lower creatures with her in her canticle. Nor is it strange that she should repeat each day in many ways the idea which runs through the canticle of creatures, sung by the youths in the furnace of Babylon, and so touchingly and mystically repeated by the loving heart of Saint Francis of Assisi and sung by his saintly lips.

When things are thus viewed, the Church is seen as a stream of purity and benediction for the material world. She is, then, a regal way through which these material creatures, lacking intelligence and will, mysteriously rise and climb to spiritual heights. Though devoid of intelligence and will, they are capable of submissively serving the mind and heart of the holy Spouse of Jesus Christ.

Yet the elevation and spiritualization of matter by the Church does not stop here. There is another region of light and life in which matter really enters into participation in life and trembles in the chaste desires of hearts which love God.

III

Man lives in a material world. Through his body he is in very active contact with the matter which he uses and which is embodied in his organic life. Matter, assimilated in the human organism, is not a mere material entity used by man for ends often immaterial — for example, the pen used for writing — but a truly integral part of the human body, vivified by its life and associated with it in regard to man's eternal destiny. Since man has been elevated to the supernatural order, which is a participation in the divine life, so, too, his body has been raised to these heights in its own manner. Therefore, the same holds true for the matter contained within it. On earth this matter which has been made the body of a man in grace, becomes the temple of the Holy Ghost, a member of Jesus Christ, a sacred vessel of divine gifts and a living chalice of supernatural essences. It vitally co-operates in divine works and operations. When animated by a soul in grace and moved by a will in charity, this matter aids in spreading the divine life of the soul through actions and diffusing it through word and example. And if this matter belongs to a priest of the Church, it can spread this divine life in the vast world of souls by its own immolation and sacred operations. Thus divine life penetrates matter, and in its own way assimilates it so that the latter is left sanctified.

Furthermore, through the mysterious bond of the Spirit of Jesus, who vivifies souls, men are vitally possessed by and united to Jesus and really made His mystical members. Jesus diffuses His life in them, so that they are appropriately and mysteriously established as part of the life of Jesus, who is the head of His Mystical Body. Matter, circulating in the bodies of the members of Jesus Christ, is brought close to

Jesus and is elevated to the luminous heights of the mystical
being of the Son of God made man. This marvelous union of
Jesus' mystical members is the Church. In the Church matter
attains the heights of the supernatural life. It participates
in the profound circulation of life which, issuing from the
heart of the august Trinity and passing through the sacred
spring of Christ's humanity, overflows into holy souls and
leaves its divine aroma in the bodies of the children of God.

We can now discern what the function of living matter
will be in this divine organism of the Church. It sings the
divine praises and soothes the world of the spirit with its
voice of peace and its jubilant paeans to God. It implores
the divine mercy and utters cries of penance and constraining
prayers for pardon. It weeps over the sins of men, sheds tears
and the blood of repentance, or exhausts itself in suffering
and sacrifice embraced for the sake of God. It preaches Jesus'
doctrine to men and pours the water of regeneration over those
who come to receive the dignity of children of God. It con-
firms and pardons, consecrates and blesses. It pronounces the
marvelous words which truly bring Jesus among us under the
form of the Eucharist and gives Him to us as food for our
souls. All these supernatural works are performed by living
matter animated by the Holy Spirit, who gives being and life
to the Church. This is not a purifying action such as we
previously considered in creatures incapable of knowing the
divine touch, an action that removes them from unclean contact with Satan and disposes them for receiving the divine
bounties. It is not an unconscious association of material creatures with the divine praises of the Church, with the sacred
acts of worship, or with the mysterious sacramental effusion
of the life of God in souls. It is much more than all this.
It is a true participation in the life and dignity of the sons

of God, becoming to their life in the great being of the Church. Matter, then, is living and operating in the Mystical Body of Jesus Christ.

We can climb another step and see that humble matter was elevated to the high dignity of becoming the body of the Mother of God, and was raised — as a component in the body of Christ — to the divine state of the sacred humanity. "And the Word was made flesh," says Saint John, "and dwelt among us."[5] Here we see that matter created by God had to enter vitally into the sacred humanity and there remain divinized and now glorified in Jesus Christ. Could this dust of the earth, from which God formed the body of the first man with His blessed hands in the fresh and virginal springtime of the world, have received a higher honor?

From these sacred heights, pervaded by the splendor and glory of the Incarnate Word, Jesus mysteriously draws His mystical members, that they may enter into the light of glory where He is forever blessed and glorified. His members who are formed amid the hardships of life will reach these heights of eternal bliss if they remain faithful to the end. Not only the soul, but also the body, will participate in this glorious life. The soul will have the better part. Yet out of its riches it will bestow ineffable happiness on the body, making it incorruptible and glorious, agile and spiritualized. Thus the body will be a living and docile instrument of the soul and an integral part of the glorified members of Christ. Matter, then, will have reached in and through the Church the summit of its splendor; it will have bathed in the waters of God's river which rejoices and beatifies the eternal city of the saints.

As a habitation for regenerated and glorified humanity, God will fuse the heavens and the planets, changing them

---

[5] John 1:14.

into a new heaven and a perfect world fitted to the glorious children of God who have come home. Creation was pure and splendid when it came forth from the hand of God. It is still marvelous, filled with the divine principle, and sustained by divine love, in spite of the horrible sins which mar and partially destroy it. Yet, when it is renewed by the divine power as a home and a fatherland for the blessed human society, it will have attained that degree of spirituality, of light and beauty, which Divine Love planned for the eternally glorious dominion of Jesus.

No human power is capable of elevating the material world to such heights. Civilization, no matter how much it learns of the riches of matter, no matter how much it exploits them by unusual inventions, will never be able to reach even the foot of this holy mountain of glory. There the Church, by sanctifying men and the lower creatures, can elevate in Christ this humble earth on which we tread and these things which love of God has put at the service of mankind.

CHAPTER II

THE CHURCH AND MAN

A MONG all God's creatures there are none whose bonds with the Church are deeper and more numerous than those of man. The visible organism of the Church on earth is composed of men. They, together with the angels, will be the living members of the Church in eternity.

We have said something during the course of this work about the action of the Church on man. We shall now complete the outline we have drawn up in this regard with a consideration of man's relationship with the Church and a brief summary of the Church's action on man.

I

In the plan of creation men are called by God to be members of the Church. It is the will of our Saviour, says Saint Paul, that "all men . . . be saved and . . . come to the knowledge of the truth."[1] The cold, harsh doctrine of Jansenism, transferring to the heart of God the narrow egoism of the human heart, claimed that the Redeemer had died, not for all men, but only for the predestined. The Church indignantly rejects this paltry and despicable teaching, which puts arbitrary limits on the merciful love that accepted even death on the cross in order to save what had been lost.[2] All men without exception are called to the dignity of children of God and members of Jesus Christ, since Jesus died for all and obtained of the Divine Mercy pardon and grace for all. If they do not all

---

[1] I Tim. 2:4.   [2] Cf. Luke 19:10.

succeed in possessing it, it is because of ill-will and human indolence, not because of failure on the part of Divine Goodness, which has exhaustively used every means that no one might lack the vivifying touch of divine love.

The Church has received from her Divine Founder the mission of teaching and sanctifying all men, as well as governing those who accept her faith and enter her society. After He had risen from the dead, just before leaving this world for His Father, Jesus said to His apostles: "All power in heaven and on earth has been given to Me. Go, therefore, and make disciples of all nations, baptizing them in the name of the Father, and of the Son, and of the Holy Spirit, teaching them to observe all that I have commanded you; and behold, I am with you all days, even unto the consummation of the world."[3] Speaking of the same command given by Jesus to His disciples, Saint Mark adds these words of the Master: "He who believes and is baptized shall be saved, but he who does not believe shall be condemned."[4] Jesus' will is final and comminatory. The Church receives the commission to teach and baptize all men; men are bound to embrace the doctrine preached by the Church and to receive Baptism, which makes them members of this divine society. Voluntary resistance to this divine call is punished by the condemnation pronounced by Jesus Christ.

Two very important truths are put into clear relief in these words of the Lord. First, the Church has the mission, and therefore the right, to teach all men and to incorporate them into her social organism. Second, all men without exception are bound to enter the Church through the door of Baptism, properly instructed in the faith. Such is the duty of every man with regard to the Church, and such is the duty of the Church

---

3Matt. 28:19-20.   4Mark 16:16.

regarding man. Man may listen or not to the word of God announced by the Church, accept or reject what is proposed to him. But he cannot renounce the duty which objectively binds him to the society of souls in Jesus Christ, nor exempt himself without guilt from its fulfillment.

This being so, there is no human power that has the legitimate authority to impede or constrain the mission of the Church, or to dissuade men from fulfilling their obligation of embracing the faith and becoming members of Christ's Mystical Body. This is, we repeat, the Church's right with regard to men, as well as the duty of every child of Adam in regard to the Church.

Now we must note three positions which men occupy with regard to the Church: (1) those who have not entered the Church; (2) those who are in the Church; (3) those who have separated from the Church because of heresy, schism, apostasy or who have been excommunicated. The first group are obliged to incorporate themselves in the Church from the moment when, having been correctly informed about this supernatural mystery, they realize their obligation in regard to it. The second group must remain in the Church and have no legitimate moral liberty to separate themselves from her. The third group, though separated from the Church, is yet obliged to re-enter her organism and live her life. To the first group the Church preaches her doctrine and manifests her divine rights, in order that they may accept her authority and become incorporated into her society. She gently energizes and urges the second group, so that they may advance in the spiritual life which so abundantly flows from her being and circulates throughout her Body. The Church urges and advises the third group of men to subject themselves again to obedience to her, casting away whatever has separated them from the maternal bosom. Those who have once been properly informed about the Church, but who obstinately refuse to enter this divine society of souls or to become reintegrated into her life, become liable to the terrible judgment of Jesus Christ. Those who are seeking God with a pure intention, yet through invincible ignorance fail to recognize their duty towards the Church — whether they be infidels, or born in and educated in heresy or schism in good faith — will not lack the grace of truth, which God gives in secret ways, that He may sanctify them and unite them with the true Church.* It is impossible for a soul in grace not to possess the Holy Spirit in a vital manner. And it is impossible to possess the Divine Spirit without being in the Church — that is, the vast multitude of souls supernaturally vivified by Personal Love. Only God, who understands and penetrates the secrets of human hearts, knows who culpably resists the truth or who maliciously excludes it. Only God, who loves men intimately and desires that all of them should be saved, knows the paths through which grace is directed to souls and to the hearts which sincerely seek Him among the shadows of error into which they were born and among which they were reared. Sooner or later the Lord rewards this noble effort in the pursuit of truth with the life of grace, which sanctifies and incorporates these souls, without their knowledge, into the most vital part of the Church. And often God rewards them with the knowledge of the Church as the one true Church in which, through Baptism, they can find the spiritual promised land they are seeking.

With regard to the actual members of the Church, we must say that their obligation to her is by no means limited

---

*TRANSLATOR'S NOTE. Fray Colomer's wording here has been recast in view of the content of the encyclical of Pius XII, *Mystici Corporis,* paragraph 61, which reads: " ... as Christ is the Head of the Church, so is the Holy Spirit her soul. The original of Fray Colomer's text here read: " ... unite them with the invisible soul of the Church."

to their not leaving her by committing a mortal sin which would separate them from her as dead members are segregated from a living organism. The Church is not like a city or a civil society from which one can legitimately depart by changing his abode or going to live in another country. Nor is she like a recreational society, in regard to which it is enough to pay one's dues or to fulfill a prescribed formality in order to remain a member in good standing. Rather, the Church is a living organism with a physical life — what everyone calls physiological life she truly possesses through the vivifying presence of the Divine Spirit, who gives her a vitally profound and true unity which no other society has. Therefore, in this organism the members must be living members; they must continually grow in the life which animates the whole body and which is manifested in each individual member. A Christian cannot legitimately remain stationary in his spiritual development. If it were otherwise, it would be like saying that although the members of our body are responsible for its organic growth, they might properly remain as small as they were at birth, while the whole body advanced and reached its proper stature. The Church will permit these vicious atonies on the part of many of her members. Yet no one can dispense himself from growing in Jesus Christ. Rather, everyone is subject to the internal law and the deep-seated exigency of his supernatural constitution, which is in all things to grow in Jesus Christ until he has reached the fullness of spiritual being which God desires for him.

A double right flows from this: (1) that of the Church to oblige her members to fulfill their duties, as well as to incite them to the perfection of the state in which they find themselves; (2) that of the members to co-operate with the spiritual aids offered by the Church, without which they cannot grow in their life as children of God. Since these aids are not given automatically but through the ministry of the members ordained for this task, who are free to fulfill their duty or not, we clearly see the grave and pressing obligation of these ministerial members not to deprive souls of the means of life that God has put into their hands. Nor are they to give sparingly of what Jesus has desired all to have in abundance.[5] Fortunately, diligent zeal and a super-excellent solicitude for the Christian formation of souls never lag in Holy Mother Church, although her ministerial members do not always give what they can and should give by means of a fervent and intense spiritual life. Yet, Divine Providence governs the world and brings its sanctifying action to souls in such a way that when they are steadfast in trials and faithful under difficult circumstances, they come forth all the more enhanced and enriched by these very difficulties. The Church provides the supernatural environment for each Christian soul; it is, besides, the immortal organism wherein the life of the individual member takes root and from which it draws strength to live.

Finally, there are souls who, having been baptized in the Church, after they have attained the use of reason break away from her through apostasy, heresy, or schism. This happens either because they fall into these spiritual aberrations through error or hardness of heart, or both; or because they consciously adhere to the heresy or schism into which they were born. In the last case it often happens that they are in good faith even when in error. Among these souls there are not lacking those who seek God with rectitude and simplicity. For such souls of good will there will not be lacking the internal touch of the heavenly Father, who will purify and vivify them with the great gift of the Spirit of

---

[5] Cf. John 10:10.

Love, who vitally incorporates them in the Church in some manner;* and they may even experience the sweet providential action which allows them actually to enter the Church as members of her visible social organization. This is likely in the case of those who are born into a Christian sect and who are of good faith and without any obstinate attachment to error. Although desiring to please God, they find themselves inculpably in heresy or schism, or separated from the Church through the apostasy of their parents. The case is very different with regard to those who, having been born and educated in the Church, voluntarily break away from her because of some pretext that could never be legitimate or some reason that could never be valid. Such a violent separation cannot take place in a Christian who humbly and with good will seeks God, and who accepts the action of Divine Providence which is latent but present even in the strangest and most disconcerting trials of life. Now, in what position do those men find themselves who have either culpably left the Church into which they were born or who have willfully adhered to the error in which they were educated?

Through validly received Baptism they are members of the Church as a supernatural visible society which has the power to demand their submission to her faith, their worthy reception of her sacraments, and their docile acceptance of her authority. The error in which they persist makes them unworthy of the Church's benefits but does not lessen her authority over them, nor does it do away with their duty to live as becomes healthy members of the Mystical Body of Christ. Baptism imprints an indelible character on the soul of men. Thus as long as he remains in this world, he must

---

*TRANSLATOR'S NOTE. See note on p. 26. The author's original text above read: " . . . incorporates them in the soul of the Church."

operate according to his ineffaceable status as a Christian by pursuing the supernatural life which only in the Church is lived completely and in an orderly way according to God. A baptized person cannot cast off his Christian character or break the bond of his dependence on the only legitimate and binding supernatural society in the world. Neither can the Church lose her status as the Mother of such souls, nor her rights over them. When one of her unfortunate sons is converted, it is not necessary for the Church to baptize him again in order to incorporate him once more. Rather, the prodigal son renounces his errors, and the Church pardons him by lifting her prohibition with regard to his participation in her sacred gifts.

A comparison will put into clear relief the difference in the relationship of these separated members to the Church and that of those who have never been members. In order to make her rights effective, the Church could have recourse to force, as civil societies do. She could apply it to the baptized who have rebelled against her divine authority through apostasy, heresy, or schism. Yet she could not use it against infidels who, although obliged to be Catholics by a decree of God, still are not her subjects. (Infidels will answer to God concerning their resistance to the divine call of the Church if they have formed their conscience concerning it.) But the separated members of the Church are still responsible to the Church. She justly deprives them of the spiritual possessions to which they had a right through Baptism; they have become unworthy of these because of their separation from the divine society founded by Jesus Christ on the primacy of Peter and on the Apostolic college and continued in the catholic, apostolic, and Roman Church.

Such are, in brief, the concrete relations existing between the Church and the three classes of men in the world. All the children of Adam are called by God to enter this holy ark, outside which there is no salvation.* All have the duty of being children of the Church and of living her life from the moment they are sufficiently informed about her. No one is morally free to fulfill this duty or not at his own good pleasure, nor to arbitrarily enter or leave this divine society of the children of God, as one can, for instance, relinquish one's civic affiliation and become incorporated into another, a different civic society. The Church is the only obligatory supernatural society for men. Its obligation is imposed upon them by one who has all power in heaven and on earth. Those who follow the divine call and hence do not wish to sin against the interior light that "enlightens every man who comes into the world," and who thereby accept the faith and the life of the Church, will be saved. Those who close their ears to the voice from heaven which calls them to live as children of God in the Church, will be condemned. There is no human power that can invalidate the firm word of Jesus Christ, nor take from the Church the right to seek all men, no matter where they are, so that she can teach them about the faith and draw them to her, making them sons of God and educating them as members of Jesus Christ, brothers of the Redeemer and co-heirs with Him of the life and glorious heritage of the heavenly Father. The right of the Church to effect the salvation of men lies in the living word of God, and not in the variable contingencies of earthly powers.

II

Along with the universal right of the Church to man's submission to her spiritual empire, there is also the unlimited influence of her action on man's life. Nor is the influence of

---

*TRANSLATOR'S NOTE. See p. 26.

the Church confined to the frontiers of time. Rather, it reaches invisibly into eternity, by means of the Church's action through the communion of saints in heaven and in purgatory, whose members are the permanent fruits of her vital action, the souls that continually rise from the visible society of the Church in time to the invisible one of eternity.

There is another difference between this supernatural society of souls and highly developed natural societies, in regard to communication with the invisible world of those who have departed from this life. Human societies preserve the memory of their illustrious men, as an example, a stimulus, and a source of common admiration for their compatriots. If their memory is effaced from the minds of their fellow citizens, they lose all influence over them and thus remain no more than a faded memorandum in an archive, with no direct power over the generation which has forgotten their name. Those souls who pass from the visible Church to the invisible, whether they be renowned in the minds of men or unknown, remain a living power in action on behalf of the Church on earth. An intense current of life rises from earth to heaven, and from those regions flows back to this humble abode of the children of God in formation. The transcendent being of the Church is the reason for this and for the profound difference on this point, as on many others, between the Church and human societies. However, it is not our intention here to touch on this aspect of the Church's life, since we have treated it in a previous book.[6] Here it is our purpose to put into clear relief, with regard to the individual man, the Church's action in raising his dignity and developing his conscience.

---

[6]*The Catholic Church: The Mystical Body of Christ*, (Paterson, N. J.: St. Anthony Guild Press, 1952).

In effect, with her doctrine and her practice, the Church is an eminent institution working for the rehabilitation and elevation of human dignity. Man, in the eyes of the Church, is not a creature thrown into an existence amid the assaults of the struggle for life, nor is he the flower of the spirit which opens here one day and then quickly fades and disappears, leaving but scanty trace of himself on the feeble memory of the living. Rather, in the eyes of the Church, man is a being who possesses a free, intelligent, and immortal soul. He is a person responsible for his acts, which have an eternal significance — a person who comes from God and must return on the wings of intellect and love to Him, his final end and his glorious and beatific reward, if he is to achieve his divine destiny.

Furthermore, God calls him to the eminent dignity of being both His son and a member of Jesus Christ, destined to a life of grace and its glorious fruition in heaven. The Church is the Mother of the children of God, the divine organism in which they are true members, animated by the Holy Spirit and invisibly directed by Jesus Christ as the Head of His Mystical Body. The Church also teaches — with assured certainty in her teaching, which is the infallible affirmation of mysterious truths — that Divine Goodness has given each one of these fragile human creatures a good angel. This angel invisibly guards, protects, and helps his earthly charge on the difficult paths of life and on the spiritual ascent to God. The Church affirms that she has received from God the treasures of the supernatural life in order to pour them abundantly upon souls who have been redeemed by Jesus Christ and who do not reject this divine abundance.

Man, then, in fact and in the estimation of the Church, is a son of the heavenly Father, a member and brother of Jesus Christ, a living temple of the Holy Ghost, an heir of the glorious vision of God, which is the supernatural life clearly seen and beatifically possessed. In the eyes of the Church man is of divine origin and has a noble destiny to fulfill in the world in order to enjoy the plenitude of eternity. This does not depend on man's social status on earth, nor on his riches or natural talents. It is a general call of merciful Love who gave His life for the redemption of all and who has unlimited capacity for sanctifying all and securing for them the fulfillment of their supernatural destiny, if they do not willfully refuse to co-operate in this divine work. The Church preaches this doctrine and affirms these mysterious truths for the benefit of all men, not as the patrimony of a spiritual aristocracy, but for the destitute and unfortunate as well as for those endowed with worldly goods.

A doctrine which thus elevates and ennobles man and which places him in the splendor of divine light, is not compatible with what seeks to drag man down to the level of beasts and makes of him an animal with refined appetites and abilities and with less restraint in fixed and regulated instincts. In regard to the sanctification of souls and the formation of children of God, it makes little difference to the Church whether men are rich or poor, happy or disconsolate, powerful or weak.[7] All are called by God's mercy to participate in the divine life and in the high dignity of members of God's family, to have an ineffable and vital relationship with the Father, the Son and the Holy Spirit. Is there any higher equality among men, any brotherhood more profound, any liberty more august than this, the right to be and to live as a child of God and a brother of Jesus Christ? What are the inequalities of man in the light of this high dignity which all men can attain merely by the fact that they are mem-

---

[7]Cf. Gal. 3:28.

bers of the Church and thus have at their disposal the abundant treasure of doctrine and life which Jesus has entrusted to His Spouse, that it may be a patrimony of all men who seek to profit by it?

This doctrine has been sown in the depths of human spirit. It has been firmly upheld without error by unceasing preaching and corroborated by practices which make it part of life. Of necessity, in coming into living contact with this doctrine, the opprobrium of slavery, the oppression of the helpless, and whatever hinders the legitimate betterment, the spiritual and material progress of the poor and needy, must gradually disappear. And this in spite of the tenacity with which errors converted into customs and sustained by special interests have entrenched themselves in society. There still is much to be done in this regard. The condition does not exist because of any negligence on the Church's part in inculcating her doctrine and condemning the unjust use of power and the cold egoism of those who exploit the poorer classes. Rather, it is due to the fact that custom and egoism raise a solid wall blocking the penetration of the Church's life, which is charity. Hence it cannot enter into the life of the wealthy as a class, or the social actions of those possessing power. The pagan heartlessness of these privileged classes has aroused the hatred of the less fortunate thus victimized by inhuman provocation and exploitation. And out of the strife of these two tremendous forces not dominated by religion — which in practice both have forgotten — arise the violent convulsions which threaten to pulverize the social order, and to make peaceable human relations impossible. If the Church should disappear from the world and if the light of her doctrine were extinguished in the hearts of men, it would not be long before we returned to monstrous pagan morals. Life would then be converted into a bloody banquet, in which the more powerful would inhumanly devour the weak. There would be no respect for human dignity and no consideration for the immortal destiny of men. Although human pride may deny the Church and ignorant irreligious forces may blaspheme her, she is the only infallible and uplifting power in the world. And she continues to sustain the world without yielding to or relinquishing the formidable weight of corrupt nature, as she transforms the value of things and inspires a true appreciation of man's destiny in time and in eternity.

Another constant, beneficial, and profound influence which the Church has on men is the development and purification of the individual conscience. Her doctrine is not only an orientation of life which is externally manifested by actions. It is a doctrine whose rays also penetrate the innermost corners of the heart, so as to illumine it and thus put order and purity into the secret sources of conscious life. Jesus, in His admirable Sermon on the Mount, touched the very depths of man's heart with His moral injunctions. Hence He demanded rectitude, temperance, order, and moral uprightness in those deep regions whence spring thoughts and affections that become embodied in external actions and thus exert their salutary or poisonous influence. Jesus is not satisfied with an apparently well-ordered and godly life, if this life does not exist also within the depths of the heart. Hence He said: "Not everyone who says to Me, 'Lord, Lord,' shall enter the kingdom of heaven; but he who does the will of My Father in heaven shall enter the kingdom of heaven. Many will say to Me in that day 'Lord, Lord, did we not prophesy in Thy name, and cast out devils in Thy name, and work many miracles in Thy name?' And then I will declare to them, 'I never knew you. Depart from Me, you workers of iniquity.'"[8]

8Matt. 7:21-23.

Moral life begins in the conscience and is then manifested outwardly by visible acts. Man's life is not limited to what he does publicly as a member of society. Rather, it develops in the intimacy of the family circle and in the much more secret realm of the mind and heart. The moral law embraces all life, private and public, what can be seen and what cannot. And divine judgment concerns the whole of life; no force which operates in the human conscience and influences action escapes evaluation with regard to its action and worth. The Church therefore educates her children, forms their conscience, and compels them to be careful of the smallest and most hidden movements of their heart.

Furthermore, if the Church had only the power of her teaching in her arduous task of moral improvement of conscience and human life, she would certainly be destroyed in her conflict with our wounded and fallen nature. The dead weight of human weakness is not lifted with only beautiful and elevated moral teachings, nor is man's moral betterment effected, except in rare cases of outstanding generosity and naturally high-minded souls.

Coming from God, the Church's teaching has a mysterious uplifting force which can transform life from the ordered and modest existence of a good Christian to that of the spiritual heroism of sanctity. Habitual grace — which is the life of God engrafted in the soul in order to divinely animate man — and actual grace — which is the help of God in doing good, power in weakness, light in darkness, stimulus to good in time of apathy, fear of evil, desire for perfection — are divine urges which awaken, enliven, and sustain man's moral energies in the noble task of living according to God. By means of grace, Jesus resides in the soul as a model to be imitated during life.

The teaching of the Church, infallibly explained and developed by her, points like a finger to what the soul must do in order to achieve this imitation of Christ and to live this life. God's gentle and secret pressure mortifies the passions, stimulates good sentiments, keeps us from foolishly straying into the path of evil, and compels us to walk along the right road. Thus it incessantly sustains the individual activity of one who desires and strives to fashion himself according to Jesus Christ, or better, who allows himself to be molded by the Divine Artificer as He sculptures the living statue of a child of God.

The sacraments of Penance and the Holy Eucharist play an important part in this work of spiritual formation. The first, besides the grace it gives to those who receive it worthily, is a permanent moral school suited to the nature and needs of the individual. The penitent examines his conscience and scrutinizes all the corners of his heart in order to clearly manifest his needs to the one who can pardon him in the name of God and thus help him to improve. The second places the soul in a sacred and mysterious contact with Jesus which operates in those who receive Him worthily as the food of eternal life. The spiritual power and moral vigor which these two sacraments place in well-disposed souls, are incalculable. To evaluate them, it would be necessary to know through experience what the world and souls would be without them and what, in spite of human misery, men finally attain with such sacraments.

Only the Church possesses this capacity for elevating and renewing man's life. Her doctrine of truth is accompanied by a restorative and uplifting force; and both, the power of grace and the light of doctrine, are a perpetual force in behalf of the moral elevation of the regenerated human family. When to the efficacy of the Church's action is joined the generous co-operation of Christian souls, advancement is prodigious, and its effects reach marvels of moral renovation and betterment; in human society this is brought about by the saints.

In lives thus purified and well-ordered, every noble aspiration finds a propitious environment in which to develop; every spiritual activity, a stimulus and spur to action. Legitimate human relationships, both private and public, sincere respect for order and the authority which maintains it, the noble disposition of the mind to penetrate the mystery of things by means of science, to delve, through art, into the lofty regions of beauty with regard to the good, beneficial, and exquisite things man can do when moved by its inspiration or stimulated by human relationships — all these actions find a healthy and sunny climate in consciences purified by a Christian life that is deeply experienced and seriously practiced.

The Church causes regenerated men to be aware of their eminent dignity as sons of God. She calls upon them all to possess this dignity, and she gives them the power to wear it proudly before their own eyes and those of the world. Hence she is the most powerful constructive and progressive force the world has ever known. The foolish struggle carried on by earthly powers against the Church can be explained only by mysterious hatred on the part of the enemy of mankind and by the blind pride of his helpers on earth.

CHAPTER III

THE CHURCH AND THE FAMILY

NATURAL societies are not members of the Church in the strict sense of the word. To be such they would have to be incorporated in the social being of the Church as integral members born of her supernatural fruitfulness. Yet these societies can be illumined by her doctrine, invigorated by her ethics, and their religious obligations regulated by her liturgical norms. There is, then, a notable difference between religious associations, which are entirely dependent on ecclesiastical authority for their being and operation, and natural societies, which can operate legitimately in their sphere independently of the Church's authority; between the relationship of man to these societies and to the supernatural Catholic society. Man is meant to live as a member of this latter society. It is intended that natural societies should develop in such a way as to be inspired and animated by the holy teaching and divine influence of the Church to the degree that they are able to receive it.

Among these societies the family is the one which most deeply receives the Church's vivifying action, since it is based on marriage, which, among Christians, when it is legitimate, is necessarily a sacrament.

First, we shall consider the juridical relationship of the family to the Church; then we shall treat of the Church's uplifting influence in the family.

I

Since creation has been elevated to the supernatural order, it is impossible that any creature should reach the fullness of its being outside this order, in which God has included all things. Therefore, neither man nor natural societies can reach the acme of their moral perfection outside the divine plan, living only in the natural order and paying attention only to their natural ends without any regard for their relationship to God.

When this law is applied to the family, it cannot be denied that the latter's perfection is not attained in the natural order. The family, in order to fulfill its divine vocation, must grow in the supernatural atmosphere of the Church, the only society in which there is given in its completeness the supernatural order desired by God. Therefore the family cannot be unmindful — as if it were an arbitrary affair — of this relation which the universal order established by God imposes upon it with regard to the Church.

We repeat here the three different positions in which men are found in regard to the Church. The individual family may never have entered the Church, or it may have been in the Church, or it may have severed its connections with the Church. In each of these situations there is present the obligatory relation arising from the universal order of things. Yet it is shown in a different way in each case.

God has not left it to man's choice whether or not he would fulfill what has been universally established by Him. But He wishes man to use his liberty properly by submitting himself to God's sovereign authority. Of itself the supernatural order is obligatory for all men, that is, for men individually and for society. There is not, nor can there be, a human association, necessary or free, permanent or transitory, which can legitimately be established and develop without any relation to God and without any connection with the supernatural order — as if such an order did not exist or did not transcend human life. Each society must adjust itself to this order in the way which its mode of being demands and the ends to be achieved require. No society has a right to be governed interiorly or to direct its natural activity in opposition to the supernatural order. Nor may it place obstacles to its members' living as children of God in the Church. The family is not excepted from this sacred obligation. God, the Author of nature, has established the family on the institution of marriage for the preservation of mankind. And He has raised matrimony, as a source of grace, to the dignity of a sacrament, in order to increase the number of children of God, and that the family may be a sure channel through which the life of the Church can easily reach souls. Hence, so that it may be well ordered and fulfill the divine plan, the family must be based on Christian marriage and must regulate all its action according to the doctrine of Holy Mother Church. A non-Christian family, naturally constituted and governed by the dictates of reason, is an incomplete entity, incapable of fulfilling its divine mission in the world. A Christian family separated from the Church is something dislocated and poorly anchored in the order of things as God wants them. According to the divine order, the family must be Catholic and must live entirely in accord with the norms and graces of the Church.

It follows from this fact that the non-Christian family has no right to prevent its members from embracing the Catholic faith. The husband cannot take this right from his wife, nor can she take it from him. Parents may not impede their sons in this regard, nor can the latter oppose the conversion of the former. Masters may not curtail their servants' action to embrace the true faith. By divine decree every family and its members are obliged to be Catholic. Hence it is impossible that any one of its members should be permitted to impede the others from fulfilling the will of God and entering into the order established by Him. No human power has the right to stop the Church from spreading the light of her teaching and scattering the seeds of her life throughout the world, that their influence might reach the family hearth. This right of souls to the life of grace in the Church is irrevocable. Thus, if one of two pagan spouses embraces the faith, and if he or she does not find in the other a respect for his or her belief nor a guarantee of liberty as a child of God, the converted spouse may — as St. Paul teaches — legitimately be separated from the infidel by breaking the matrimonial bond, which must not be a thing of tyranny and danger for the one converted to God.[1]

Neither have pagan parents the right to impede the conversion of their children when the latter, having attained the use of reason and having been sufficiently instructed in the faith, desire to embrace the faith. The obligation to enter the Church is universal. There is no reason that can cancel this obligation, no human power which can legitimately oppose it. From the moment this duty shines clearly in one's conscience, no one nor any thing has the power to exempt from it one who knows that God calls all to the knowledge of the truth and to the shelter of the one ark of salvation on the stormy sea of life.

With regard to children who have not yet attained the use of reason, the Church has the right to draw them to herself through the consent and good will of their parents or guardians. However, she has not the right to sanctify the children by violently snatching them away from paternal au-

---

[1] I Cor. 7:12-16.

thority, that they may be educated in the faith away from the
latter. Parents are responsible to God if they make bad use
of their authority with regard to their children on such an
important and transcendent point as this. The Church has
no power to break natural bonds between children and their
parents, nor has she any reason to impose her authority violently upon those who reject it. She never forces her doctrine
on those who have sufficient intelligence to accept it freely.
Neither does she impose her law on children whose parents
do not respect the Christian life which the baptized must
live. Such parents will render an account to God for their
resistance, as will those who, though urged on by the truth
of faith, have not subjected themselved to it nor acknowledged
its right to govern human life.

With regard to children of families outside the Church who
are placed in danger of death, Holy Mother Church can assert her right to save them, baptizing them without fear or
regard for the protests of parents. The blindness of the latter
is no reason why these souls in the critical moment of passing
into eternity, should enter it dispossessed of divine grace and
thereby forever excluded from the kingdom of God which
Jesus gained for us all by the shedding of His blood. In
this fearful and decisive moment the right of the Church
prevails. It is not left to the parents whether their dying children will or will not receive Baptism, which when received
opens the door of heaven to them.

The Church can assert her right to incorporate children
before they reach the use of reason when their parents or
guardians, or one of them, consents to their Baptism and offers
guarantees to respect the child's Christian education. And this
holds with greater reason in regard to abandoned children
who have no one in the world to defend them. The Church

mercifully gathers these buds of human life and sanctifies them with baptismal grace,[2] making them sons of God and flowers of the eternal paradise.

In a word, the family must necessarily live in the supernatural order of the Catholic Church. It has a duty, as a society, to enter this order and within it to develop its natural activities.

With these things understood, every family is meant for the Church, and the Church has a right to bring to the family the light of her teaching and the holy influence of her life. This obligation ought to be fulfilled by every family, and especially is it binding upon the head of the family, who bears this responsibility before God and before the world of the diminutive society of the home. The family may remain in the darkness of error outside the Church because of the willful and obstinate resistance of all the members or of the family head. In such a case, the holy Spouse of the one who died to save us seeks no other exercise of her right over souls than to pray that God in His mercy may draw these wayward societies to the light of the truth. The Church does not use violence to enforce her rights over these souls. Rather, she only mourns and grieves for them and thus uses a sweet violence against merciful Love with her prayers, that these souls may be led to the sheepfold of the Good Shepherd and the maternal warmth of His Holy Spouse. If she does not achieve this, the Church can withdraw without hatred or bitterness, and thus leave to divine mercy and justice the lot of those she cannot resuscitate by the generous zeal of her apostolate, the ardor of her prayers, and the power of her sacrifice.

---

[2]Cf. *Codex juris canonice*, canons 750 and 751.

II

Having noted the juridical relationship of the family with the Church, we must now consider the action of the Church on the family that accepts her teachings. Here we must also note the paternal direction of the Church's authority in all that concerns God, the Christian formation of the family members, and the influence of her supernatural life.

There is no natural society which the Church's action penetrates more deeply than the family. It begins in matrimony, which among Christians is a sacrament. A child of the Church is much more than a human person: he is a child of God indelibly marked with the sacred character of Baptism. By the will and edict of Jesus Christ, conjugal union among Christians is not a mere natural contract, one and indissoluble for the ordered propagation of mankind. Rather, it is a sacrament which gives a sacred character to the matrimonial contract, confers grace on the well-disposed contracting parties, and supernaturally aids them in extending the kingdom of God by the addition of new members. The profound life of the Church flows into the family through the channel of this divine sacrament which, besides having an intrinsic value and action, is a symbol of the holy union between Christ and His Spouse the Church. The Church's action in Christian marriage is not only regulative but also vivifying. The grace which immanently resides in the Spouse of Christ because of the vital presence of the Holy Spirit is truly communicated to the well-disposed married couple and does develop their divine life. At the same time it gives them a most certain right to the supernatural aids necessary to discharge in a saintly way the duties of the married state and to educate in a Christian way the children God gives them.

Although the family is a society placed in time and one which with time passes, through holy matrimony we see it become rooted in the Church whose life is for eternity. The Christian family is the Church's offspring, although it is of transitory existence and function. It is a natural society elevated to divine heights for the formation of the children of God and as a help to its members in achieving their perfection as members of Jesus Christ. The Christian who remains faithful to the end during the time of earthly trial will be forever a member of Christ in His glorious Mystical Body. When the Christian family has completed its mission on earth, it can look forward to an eternal resurrection and restoration which it does not now possess. In heaven there will be a very delicate intimacy and a comforting bond between members of families. All the natural and lawful bonds which unite hearts in love will remain a permanent tie of charity and a pleasing taste of glory for those who sanctified them and used them for the fulfillment of the divine order in creation.

Once the sacred fount of graces from Christian marriage is open to the family, the latter's moral and spiritual improvement is certain and abundant. Of course, this supposes the co-operation of family members with the grace of God and their sincere submission to the teachings and laws of the Church.

Christian spouses conscious of their dignity are able to maintain their fidelity inviolable and to respect themselves chastely as temples of the Holy Spirit. How much can be gained, by way of nobility of sentiments, purity of association, and rectitude of intentions, through the intimate communication of Christian spouses! The grace of God comes down upon them like a sacred veil; it clothes them with temperance and gives them the strength that fortifies them against the regrettable weaknesses surrounding that instinct which more than any other seems to have felt the blow of original sin and the deprivation of primitive integrity. Their love is refined and spiritualized. And when these sense perceptions lose the incentive which has nourished them, Christian spouses find higher and more permanent motives which keep alive the flame of love in hearts that do not know old age.

Souls thus forged by religion and interiorly nurtured by grace do not shrink before sacrifice. Rather, they generously embrace it and in a holy manner stimulate each other in their task of carrying the burden of family life. They never willfully and egotistically shut off the fountains of life, seeking the enervating satisfaction of blind appetite outside God's law. Rather, they embrace matrimony with all its consequences, and since their hope in God is firm, they are able to bring honor to His name and the dignity of Christians united before God and the Church to procreate children for heaven. Who could estimate the acts of self-renunciation and whole-hearted generosity, of sacrifice and holy resignation to the will of God, of stalwart surrender to Providence, of fervent prayer and of supernatural elevation of the heart in Christian spouses who are able to act in this way in the intimacy of married life? Will they cease to be pleasing to the eyes of God when their lives are fused into one by chaste love and immolated in a Christian manner on the altar of conjugal duty? Could they do less than draw down upon their family circle divine blessings, like a shower of fresh roses from the eternal paradise?

Such spouses need and find in the life of the Church the strength required to remain faithful in their vocation and firm in their holy duties as Christian spouses. In the Church they find the wide and powerful vein of grace which strengthens and rejuvenates them from within, even when time has weakened their bodies and left in them the marks of old age and the ruins of enchantments which have now passed. The sacraments, liturgical prayer, the sacrifice of the Mass, the

Word of God, spiritual direction — all that the Church possesses for the benefit of souls is at work in Christian spouses. These things fortify and help them, refine their sentiments, open up new horizons which widen their sphere of life as children of God, bringing to it pleasing and immortal hopes.

The influence of the Church in the Christian family does not end here. Through parents it reaches children. The physical life of the parents is propagated through the generation of children. The spiritual life of parents is infused into their children through family education and formation. If the parents are God-fearing people, profoundly Christian, sincerely and deeply pious, their children will receive from them this overflow of spiritual life. Thus it will awaken their minds and hearts to God and lift their tender young souls to the serene regions in which the spirit is tempered by truth and love. What is not a discreet, pious, and Christian mother able to do for the children she holds in her arms? With the fine delicacy of Christian sentiments and the keen ardor of her faith, she will take care to give them what is best and purest in her soul, just as with generation and lactation she gave them the purest and the best of her physical life. She will be able to open their hearts to love of God and to deposit there the seeds of piety and devotion to Jesus and His most holy Mother, to their guardian angel, and to the blessed in heaven with whom we have the closest bond. No one is as capable as a pious mother for the task of unfolding the wings of her children towards the invisible world of divine light and helping them to learn the ways of confident communication with God. Such instructions are usually never forgotten. A mother can vividly impress them upon the child's mind. There they remain as a powerful regulating force amid the wild impetus of passions, like an invisible hand which redirects one along the proper path after he has strayed by walking along the errant ways of life.

Besides giving religious formation, parents will continue to develop the moral conscience of their children, awakening and enlivening in them sentiments of docile submission to authority, respect for their elders, reverence for consecrated persons, good will towards all, charity towards the poor and disabled, compassion for the afflicted and the unfortunate. It is impossible for parents who are established in their faith and who truly live it not to act this way towards their children. It is impossible for such parents not to function for their children as apostles, full of love and discretion, and to serve as an efficacious example of what they teach. Normally all the Christian virtues can be expected of a family illumined by faith and constantly irrigated, as it were, like a highly cultivated garden, by the stream of sacramental grace from parents who by their lives preserve their dignity as Christian spouses. In such a family the joys of the family hearth must necessarily be purer, the trials of life less bitter, its burden more admirably sustained, and exhausting crises must become an occasion of enduring confidence in the heavenly Father who never forgets his poor children in the battle of the day. The life of the family then becomes, as it were, a fabric sweetly scented with the fragrance of Jesus Christ, and the family a flower opened towards heaven, its roots in the fertile soil of the Church.

If the family is poor, it can honor poverty worthily with sanctified work, with Christian modesty of life, and with holy resignation amid inevitable privations, which it will accept as a penance or as a part of the sacrifice which molds the family members to the likeness of Jesus. No prodigality will be found in such homes, for they will be touching reflections of the peaceful family hearth of Nazareth. Religion has power to sanctify and improve all things and to make of the poor family, pressed by the needs of each hour, a tranquil pool of divine peace and a vivid example of the Christian life.

If the family has an abundance of material goods, it will know how to administer them beneficially for the other children of God who are often in such want. It will attend to its own needs with Christian moderation, avoiding superfluous luxuries or Sybaritical delicacies. Such indulgence is nothing but an insult to the poverty of one's fellows; it arouses the repressed anger of those who see themselves hungry in the face of misused plenty which, according to God's design, should benefit all.

To consider next the attitude of the Christian family toward the servants who help in the family tasks and the round of life characteristic of a prosperous home: the family will not regard as strangers these poor members of Jesus Christ whom necessity has forced to seek of them work and shelter. Still less will they look upon their servants with cold disdain and insolent pride. Accepting them, rather, as brothers in Jesus Christ, they will know how to care for their religious instruction and be solicitous for their moral improvement. They will not burden them excessively or treat them in a proud and domineering manner. They will prudently see to it that their domestic employees feel that in this family which shelters them there is a love that fills the need for affection, and a Christian zeal for their spiritual and material well-being. When this relationship is maintained in wealthy homes, the circle of Christian love receives and holds the servants with firmness and gentleness, disposing them to feel proud to spend their strength in maintaining the splendor of a family which diffuses the Christian virtues among its members. They will be glad to end their days in respected old age within a family animated by love of Jesus Christ.

There are some families which are oppressed with daily toil. These scarcely earn the bare necessities of life. And there are other families which enjoy all the comforts of life. But both types can be vivified by the life of the Church when it is sincerely put into practice. Between these two extremes, one may find the golden mean of the classes that lie in between, in all their degrees and shades. If one pours into them all, as into living vases, the rare essences of the Christian virtues, one will catch a glimpse of what family life can be when the Catholic religion is not regarded as mere etiquette or vain pretense. It can be, then, a vital contact of souls with God — through the sacraments and through the practice of a doctrine which is sacrifice made with a love and charity that find their power and delight in the cross.

In families thus penetrated with Christian ideals, every virtue has its place, and all that is good and noble in human life progresses and flourishes. Faith brilliantly illumines within the family circle every mind united in the same ideal. Love fuses the hearts which have the same feeling and desire. Religion, loved and practiced, lifts the soul with immortal hopes. These three powers open the lips of these families to Christian prayer and bring them to their knees before the Divine Majesty and Goodness, whose august and beneficent action is constantly experienced in the family like a blessing bestowed by invisible hands over a holy place sanctified by Christian life.

What is the source of this current of divine favors which, traveling through the heart of the Christian family, lifts it to the serene peace of just souls and to a sweet confidence in the providence of the heavenly Father? Whence comes this power that sustains hearts united in love and sacrifice, wills joyously governed by paternal authority, appetites moderated in a holy fear of God, and noble actions stimulated by the desire for improvement and orderly progress? From the sanctifying action of the Church generously accepted and profitably used by the members of the Christian family. When Christian homes virtuously remain in the order established by God, they cannot but enjoy the blessings which always accompany those who fear God and who lovingly subject themselves to His holy law.

Have families the right to complain that they do not receive God's favors when, among them, the love of God is scorned, the divine law is slighted, religion, if any part of it remains, is a private affair of each one or a vain pretense of relations with God? Can families complain that God does not bless them, when egotism dominates and imposes its law in the great action of the transmission of life, when the education of children is neglected, and when all the frivolities of the world are cordially welcomed? When the law of God is ejected from the conscience of a family which ought to be Christian, and when the morality of the Church does not penetrate the most deep-seated relations of this society destined by Providence to be a mold for the formation of Christians, it is not strange that family life becomes corrupted. Nor are we to be surprised that the bonds of love, authority, and respect are weakened, that egotism, mastering hearts, provokes disturbances and calamities in the family which God has blessed in the sacrament of matrimony and which He would have continued to bless, if unbridled concupiscence and the forgotten practice of religion had not driven away the benediction of the Lord.

CHAPTER IV

CHURCH AND STATE

THROUGH the logical development of our subject, we now come to a most interesting and stimulating discussion concerning the relations between Church and State. Theoretically speaking, when things are viewed in the light of truth, the teaching on these relations is simple and clear. Yet in some cases the spirit of error has confused men. On the other hand, minds which have had no desire to break with Catholic truth have not been misled.

Our task is to clarify the relations between Church and State. Thus we are going to show the beneficent action of the Spouse of Christ in a civil society which allows itself to be influenced by her doctrine and penetrated by her life and spirit.

I

The unshakable foundation of these relations consists in the elevation of men to the supernatural order and in the existence of the Church as a universal, visible, and authentic organ in this order. Once this is understood, it necessarily follows that the State has duties to God which it must fulfill in a supernatural way. Hence the State must recognize in its subjects certain conditions arising from the supernatural order; it must maintain certain indispensable relations with the society placed by God in the world for the guarantee and support of this eminent supernatural order.

Granted the divine elevation of man in and through the Church, the State cannot legitimately consider its life independently of the Church. The State cannot overlook what its relations with God impose upon it as a moral person. Nor can it ignore what its very condition demands because of its existence for the common good of its members; these, as human beings, are called to the Church, and among them are many who are children of the Church by reason of baptismal grace. The relationship already, therefore, between Church and State is established as a right of the Church which cannot be denied and as a duty of the State which must be fulfilled so that the latter does not rebel against the sovereignty of God.

In the world the natural and supernatural order are not independent of each other as, for instance, are two parallel lines which are drawn out indefinitely and can never meet. Rather, they are harmonious, interconnected, and disposed in a hierarchical order; that is, the natural order is subordinated to the supernatural. This arises from the nature of things. It develops out of the full and ordered concourse of visible and invisible creatures in regard to what constitutes their essence, with a consideration of their native powers and the laws according to which they operate and develop. The supernatural life comes as an eminent gift from Divine Bounty. It descends on the natural order as its proper subject; there it is incorporated as a reality which vitally touches and elevates intelligent creatures to participation in the life of God. Of course, this is effected only when these intelligent creatures do not withdraw from this vivifying touch. This supernatural reality orders them towards a very exalted end which will be manifested, when completely developed, in unimagined splendor and capacities that far surpass those that men possess naturally. Hence it is impossible to separate and isolate the two orders. Thus the natural order cannot be considered as if it alone existed, nor can the supernatural be considered as a golden cloud or a veil of brilliant light not having any contact with the natural order. The supernatural order is definitively the life of God communicated to man, and therefore it cannot subsist outside God or without the subject who receives it. In the visible order, this subject is man; and the authentic social manifestation of the supernatural order is the Church.

Now we must consider what is the end of the State. It is the common good of the society which it directs and governs. What elements enter into this common good? All human goods which spring from nature, nature seeks for man's sustenance and betterment. These things are attained through nature. There are other divine goods which unite us supernaturally with our final end and which must mold our whole life, in order that it may develop and be orientated towards the Supreme Good, and may be directed towards the most important end of all. Now, among all these goods, the divine are entrusted to the Church; the rest, to the State. Hence the latter cannot be exempted from a true understanding of and regard for the supernatural. Nor can it change the hierarchy of ends in human life. The first of these ends is achieved by the State's accepting the doctrinal direction of the Church; the second, by its governing with a sincere moral union with the infallible authority that has received from God the mission of directing and bringing all men to their final end.

With respect to the teachings of the Church, this moral union does not diminish the sovereignty of the State or its independence in the sphere which is peculiarly its own. Grace does not mutilate nature or diminish it to a trifle, but elevates it, directing it to a much higher end and carrying it to a much higher destiny. Therefore, whatever man may naturally seek without violating right order, and what he can attain without violating the hierachy of ends, he may desire and legitimately obtain through his ingenuity and effort. These natural aspirations cannot be suitably fulfilled except in a permanent and established society which is self-sufficient and offers a guarantee of rights, as well as a favorable environment for all the activities of those associated in it. Hence civil society is necessary, since man is elevated to the supernatural order; and equally necessary is the State, which is the supreme organized authority in civil society. Because of what comes under its natural activity, what is determined by its ends, the State is subject to no earthly authority, nor is it an integral part of another, much larger society, within which the State would be what a city or social class so constituted is in the State. This full authority of the State in whatever pertains to her is her sovereignty; and the self-sufficient society constituted in the State, that is, when crowned by the sovereign State, gives her a natural independence. Civil society, therefore — which is self-sufficient for attaining its ends and for enforcing its rights — and the State which governs it — form one body in the natural order. This complete body is independent of any other natural power; it has the right to govern itself without any outside interference. The authoritative action of the State under these conditions and in this sphere constitutes the legitimate exercise of its sovereignty.

Yet neither a self-sufficient society nor the sovereign State which governs it, is independent of God or unconnected with the supernatural order. Therefore, in what concerns the latter, the State is not independent of the only authority which has received from God the supernatural direction of life. In the ordering of its own activity, the State may not rise against religious authority, as if it were an attribute of its own natural sovereignty, and thus command its subjects without acknowledgment of or respect for the rights of the Church. In the supernatural order, the State is subject to the Church through divine command; in the natural order, it is independent and sovereign within its territory and equal in status to the states coexisting with it. This is the order established by Providence in the world. States cannot change it to their liking or evade it without rebelling against sovereign authority.

In this way, the harmonious ends, the natural and supernatural, which are interlaced in a hierarchical manner within the individual without confusion or incompatibility, are manifested in Church and State. Thus each is sovereign and independent in its own order, however much the State is subject to the Church in the religious and supernatural order. This is the indirect subordination mentioned by Catholic authors. It arises out of a hierarchy of ends, and is the objective relationship between the two powers. Both are of divine origin, although in a different way. Both were established by God for the good of man. Each one co-operates in its sphere and with its own means, in a hierarchical relation, so that all may reach the final goal to which the Lord calls them and towards which He is directing them. This is the theory concerning the two powers. It has always been proclaimed by the Church and defended by Catholic writers. All men of good will who admit the existence of the supernatural order and the divine mission of the Church cannot help but recognize and embrace this theory.

Once one has accepted the fundamental principles of this doctrine, it is impossible to refute it logically. Nor can one rationally sustain the liberal error which denies the religious subordination of the State to the Church, and affirms the supremacy of the former over the latter in every sphere of its territorial dominion. Such a doctrine necessarily implies the negation of the supernatural order as a historical fact or as a higher than natural end. It denies that the Church is a divinely instituted society in which the supernatural order is realized in a fit social organization obligatory for all men.

Since both negations may be dashed to pieces against the unshakable and firm rock of the facts, one cannot deny that the
end of the State is hierarchically subordinated to that of the
Church. Nor can one deny that the authority of the State in
the religious order is limited and is herein subject to the
Church, and that no earthly power can fulfill its mission in
the world according to the divine plan without a permanent
and sincere moral union with the spiritual power of the Church.

The independence — or better, separation — of State and
Church will be in every case the affirmation of something regrettable that has been brought about by unfortunate circumstances, something that has arisen, in short, from men's blindness or malice.* But never will it be a right situation and a
solid position based on the reality of the facts. Such a separation, besides being an absurd dislocation of things, will in

---

*TRANSLATOR'S NOTE. The reader will recognize in Fray Colomer's treat-
ment of this topic the approach of the theologian writing against the background
of the Catholic state. Where the political history has been different, theologians
have introduced other positive and valid formulas covering the actual situation. It is their position that union of Church and State is not an unalterable
exigence of Catholic principles, since in every age the Church makes a practical
adjustment to the society in which she finds herself. Cardinal Baudrillart
(1859-1942) wrote: "The relations of Church and State are not regulated in
accord with absolute, and so to speak, geometrical principles; they result from
the social and political situation and from the manner in which the Church
adapts her principles to meet it."

To summarize briefly a development which may present innumerable varia-
tions of fact and circumstances, it may be said that the separation of the civil
authority and the religious authority can be more or less violently imposed; or
it can grow naturally out of a specific national situation and history. In the
latter case, the arrangement can certainly be defensible and on occasion something more. In our own country, for example, the Church enjoys a liberty and
an untrammeled vigor of life which more than one of the Sovereign Pontiffs
have acknowledged with gratitude; while many historical commentators have
contrasted these goods with the less favorable situation which has existed at
various times in states legally "Catholic."

For a more complete development of this topic, the reader is referred to
The Two Sovereignties: The Relationship between Church and State, by Joseph
Lecler, S. J. (New York: Philosophical Library, 1952).

practice constitute tyranny of the State over the Church, and will be the negation of the universal supernatural order, even if the States does not wish to admit it.

The only legitimate relation, therefore, between both powers is one of moral union. In this union there is indirect subordination of the human to the divine and the spiritual penetration of both societies by the shaping of the earthly one according to the doctrine and ethics of the Church.

II

Let us now deduce the consequences of this doctrine. The first is that the State must recognize the full right of the Church to exist and to develop freely in the world by preaching her doctrine, administering her sacraments, and exercising authority over her subjects, the faithful. The State must also recognize the Church's right to recruit and to form the members of her hierarchy, to develop her life in religious institutions, and to possess goods for the sustenance of her priests and institutions and for the exercise of public worship and other vital functions. A complete and perfect society such as the Church ought not to lack what it needs for its existence and for the achievement of its goal. A sovereign and independent authority is not subject to any other power on earth in the free exercise of its sovereignty. Hence, either one denies the Church her status as a universal religious society with a divinely given right, or one recognizes her right to exist and grow among men within the countries of the world. To embrace the first point is to do violence to history — which proclaims the divine fact of the Church — or to the sovereignty of God who established the Church. To accept the second position is to agree to what necessarily follows as a duty of the State which recognizes the divine status of the Church.

This duty is applied in a variety of ways, or better, it is reduced to numerous particular duties; for example, that of respecting the liberty of the Church in her preaching of doctrine, her establishing of schools, formation of the clergy, the governing of her members, and the administration of her property. Therefore, the State may not confiscate this property, nor may it impede the Church in her teaching, restrict her liberty with regard to the number of her ministerial organs, tamper with the life of the religious orders and congregations, or interpose civil authority between the head of the Church and the Church's subjects. Neither may the State legislate contrary to the Church's ruling on what, by virtue of her divine mission, she regulates with sovereign authority, for instance, marriage among the faithful; nor may the State legislate against the natural law, as for instance, in the case of the unity or indissolubility of marriage. In approving divorce, the State denies what God has established as the Author of nature; and when she makes civil marriage between Christians valid, the State rises against the unchangeable doctrine of the Church, which is founded on the word of Jesus Christ.

There is no danger that this liberty of the Church, when sincerely recognized and respected in practice by the State, will be an occasion of disturbance in the State or of diminution of the State's legitimate interests. When both powers proceed in a sincere moral union, there are ways of preventing evils, of correcting abuses, of avoiding the overstepping of power. By mutual accord Church and State can help each other in their particular needs and amicably solve points of dispute between the two jurisdictions, keeping as a standard the full sovereignty of the State and the Church in their respective spheres and the submission of the State to the Church in the sphere of religious and moral authority. Never is it lawful for the State to invade the jurisdiction of the Church by legislating on what is pertinent to the religious authority or by legislating against this authority in affairs which, in varying degrees, fall under the jurisdiction of both powers. The State has always open to it the way of sincere understanding with a power which is disposed to peace with earthly authority, provided it respects what Jesus Christ has entrusted to the care of the Church and what she cannot forego without being unfaithful to her Bridegroom and Founder. On this point of fidelity the Church does not and cannot yield to the pressure of any earthly power, nor does she flinch before the threats of man. Before doing this she would allow the bodies of all her ministers and her children to be annihilated. She knows what martyrdom is. And for twenty centuries she has seen how her power has always defeated her enemies and how it has been a wall against which the attacks of her persecutors have been dashed to pieces. The force of necessity finally obliges earthly powers, notwithstanding their blindness or unbridled will, to seek accord with the Church in order to save themselves from disaster. Divine Providence constrains the authorities of the world so that, willingly or unwillingly, they must recognize the Church's right to existence and to free action among souls. They are compelled to declare by their actions that anything against the order established by God lacks solidity and permanence.

We note that this duty of the State to the Church, so fruitful in its consequences, is completed by another which is more difficult for the State to fulfill; namely, the protection and defense of the Church's right to existence and to liberty in nations which persecute her. Could a State undertake a more just and noble task than to defend the unrecognized right of the kingdom of God, which is the Church? It is just for an independent civil society to defend its rights against those who desire to trample on them. Hence it is also just for it to seek alliances which will aid it with arms in maintaining its rights. In the light of these truths, can one deny that the

Church has the same right to protection and help from earthly powers when she sees herself unjustly treated by nations which refuse to respect what is more to be respected than any earthly interests? Theoretically, there is no doubt about this. Nor can there be any doubt that on such an occasion a State must not take the lead and accomplish the task with warlike zeal. Rather, it must operate prudently at the summons of the Church, who never appeals to force to defend her rights unless she is compelled by very grave reasons and for the evident well-being of souls. This duty of the State, in brief, is expressed in the famous words of Boniface VIII's Bull *Unam Sanctam,* concerning the two powers symbolized by the two swords — "the spiritual wielded by the priesthood and the material by the powers of earth, yet 'ad nutum et de patientia sacerdotis' ";[1] that is, as Dom Gréa says, according as the priesthood employs it in the service of the supernatural order or according as it permits it in the sphere of action of the natural order.[2]

Thus we see the duties of the State towards the Church. We should note that all of them are reinforced for another reason; namely, the State's obligation to help its subjects acquire the good they by nature seek as a social unit.

Men are not slaves of the State or something that the latter can dispose of at its own will. Rather, they are rational creatures who must fulfill an important duty. This duty is that of living according to God in the Church. And to this all man's other duties or rights must be subordinated. In this duty are included all those debts which man owes to God; in the light of this duty all the goods which society seeks under the guidance of the State are regulated. Neither the

---

[1]Denziger-Bannwart, *Enchiridion symbolorum definitionum et declarationum de rebus fidii et morum,* 10th edition, no. 496.

[2]Gréa, *L'Église,* Vol. II, App. I, chapter iii

family nor any other society which takes the family into its sphere may act contrary to this fundamental duty. Nor can any law be legitimate if it abrogates man's liberty to fulfill his duty of being subject to God by living as a faithful son of the Church. Hence the State cannot deny its subjects the right to the light of the soul and the spiritual life, which are found only in the Church. The State cannot tyrannically cut off the life of the family, inhibiting it in the Christian formation of its members. Nor has it the right to stifle the religious aspirations of its subjects as they live for God within the one society which has the authentic mission of bringing men to their final end. When the State does interfere in this way, it is tyrannizing over its subjects, taking away from them inalienable rights which by natural law ought to be protected by the civil authority. The State would then be perverting the natural hierarchy of ends, subjecting to its own will what it ought to serve and protect — the right of its members to live in the Church according to the divine norms of this supernatural society. The State must not be a monstrous devourer of the legitimate liberties and natural rights of its social or individual members. Rather, it must be reason served by strength for the protection and guarantee of the rights of all, in order that each individual may fulfill in this world the destiny which Providence has entrusted to him.

Through these two topics, that of the position of the State with regard to the Church in the divine plan, and that of the duties of the State towards its members, we come to a consideration of the conduct which the State must follow in regard to the Church, that the order established by God may be maintained.

Yet these are not all the reasons which oblige the State to proceed amicably with the Church in what is common to both and to be subject to her in religious matters.

The State is a moral person with relations and duties to God. It cannot possibly sever such relations or reasonably deny these duties. The State, like all creatures, depends on God, comes from God, and exists for the fulfillment of God's designs in the human family. To deny this is to deny God and to put the State in God's place. If, then, one does not want to see it fall into the senseless delirium of the pagan State, one must admit that the State has duties to fulfill before God and that it owes Him the worship of adoration and praise. Further, one must admit that the State has to recognize God as the source of all benefits, giving Him due thanks and offering Him humble and expiatory compensation for the many public sins committed in civil society. The State can neither excuse itself from this duty nor fulfill it as it pleases. Rather, it must be performed according to the norms of the only legitimate authority in the world on religious matters, namely, the Catholic Church. Therefore, in its relations with God, the State cannot ignore the Church, but must indeed consider her in paying its religious tribute to the Giver of all good, the King of Kings and the Lord of all rulers.

The doctrine which advocates separation of Church and State, as if there were nothing in common between these two societies, or which places the Church beneath the State or makes the former subject to the latter, is a negation of the divine order in the world, an upsetting of the hierarchy of ends. Furthermore, it is a form of tyranny threatening the legitimate liberty of the Church and the children of God; and it is a proclamation of the right of force over the sacred rights of the spiritual authority placed by Jesus Christ in the world for man's salvation. To erect, in principle, such a doctrine is to throw society into the darkness of error. To carry it out in practice is to live in rebellion against order and against the sovereignty of one who judges nations as individuals and has the power to reduce to dust those nations which scorn His holy law.

III

There is now one more point for us to consider in finishing this discussion of the relations between Church and State. This is the orientation of the State and society by means of the teachings, the ethics, and the life of the Church.

The orientation of the body by the soul has often been compared to that of the State by the Church. Yet the comparison goes too far. Soul and body when joined together are one complete substance; that is, one man individually as distinct from the rest. When Church and State are morally united, they are not a whole of which the Church and State are parts. This would be the negation of both societies. How, then, are the State and civil society oriented by the Church?

In the first place, this is a doctrinal orientation, that is, a firm acceptance of the teachings of the Church by those who govern the State and by those who live in the State subject to its authority. In a final analysis, all human societies may be reduced to a body of men whose common needs and interests band them together and unite them under the authority of those who govern. Therefore, the ideas which rule society and which are the secret mainspring of collective action are rooted and sustained in the minds of individuals. The more minds an idea brings together and the more deeply it penetrates the persons who accept it, the more powerful is the collective impetus it arouses and the more robust is its force and power of action. Ideas impressed on the minds of the multitudes can elevate their sentiments, unite their wills, bring about collective action, awaken common interests. In a practical sense, ideas are like an informing soul of the multitude which accepts them and the living force which moves it interiorly in one direction or another. Let us suppose the case in which a true, sound and high-minded doctrine, sustained by an infallible authority and proposed in simple formulas which gain the acceptance of the most humble and uneducated minds, takes root in thousands of citizens united by strong social bonds. And let us suppose that this doctrine is loved, accepted, and assimilated as the light of life both by those who command and those who obey, by those who are wealthy and those who are very poor. In such a case, the acceptance of this doctrine would necessarily give rise to universal concord in collective thought and feeling in respect to what is most profound and of greatest concern for all — that is, the ordering of individual life and social life according to God's plan. This light of truth will then act as an energetic unifier of opinions, as a powerful agglutinant of wills, as an effective orientator and stimulant in regard to what society has that is most profound and fundamental — which is the proper evaluation of its end, of the hierarchy of human goods, and of the social relationships of its members. As this unity of doctrine becomes permanently established in minds, the inevitable disagreements in opinions and judgments among men will be only superficial ones. The reason for this is that a fundamental doctrine, embraced by all as the word of God, curbs the disorganizing impetus of human contention and preserves unity in principles among those who may not be unified in other things.

This first molding of society and the State by the doctrine of the Church is accompanied by another which is more vital and profound. It is moral formation; that is, the teachings of the Church put into action. Catholic doctrine is not a sterile contemplation of a system of divine truths communicated to human minds for the pleasure and solace of the spirit. Rather, it is the light of life, ordained by God to penetrate man's whole being and to shape him in the mold of divine truth. It does not stop at the surface of life so as merely to form polite men who know how to get along with others. No, it actually penetrates man's conscience. If not impeded there, it effects a deep renewal which purifies the sources of human action. The man who seriously accepts this doctrine gradually improves, so that even the innermost recesses of his heart are set in order and sanctified. The light of this accepted life not only rectifies, but also elevates what is naturally right and good, uniting the human will to the divine and putting first, as a secret source of good living, the holy and adorable will of God. Purity of conscience is then converted into action. It is then not only the aroma, as it were, of integrity and the fragrance of spiritual refinement in human society, but the promise of Christ for all and the living manifestation of the holy doctrine which has deeply penetrated one who has not rejected its beneficent influence. When this moral elevation has spread throughout the social body, it cannot help but be reflected in the standards of justice found in social life, in the customs which are the honor of nations, in the mutual social respect and high-minded submission of all to those who hold authority, under God, for the good government of society. How can it help but be manifested in an orderly human society, in the citizens' faithful fulfillment of private and public duties, in the peace and harmony that facilitate the increase and diffusion of every good which the social group possesses? The doctrine of the Church thus reaches the collective conscience and gives it its power of purifying and uplifting, and its pure Christian fragrance which checks the corruption of our fallen nature. Just as from tiny streams of water flowing down the mountainside are formed larger streams breaking into gushing springs which, united with others, make a swift moving river; so, too, from the deep-seated thoughts and feelings of thousands of citizens is formed the clear manifestation of Christian family life, from which then shoot forth, like roaring waterfalls, high-minded customs and a fruitful and orderly collective life. If those first rills of consciences are clean and pure, the social manifestations which spring from them cannot be poisonous and corrupted. To the unity of minds achieved through the sincere acceptance of the Church's doctrine is joined the unity of will and of Christian sentiment which gently yet powerfully and efficaciously leads collective life to the pure source of Catholic morals. Faith illumines the intellect with divine life; Christian morals govern with loving interior compulsion. A society which is thus illumined and whose members are thus interiorly governed is said to be molded by the Church.

Does this spiritual formation go beyond this? Undoubtedly it does.

We have already said that the Church is not a mere society with a noble philosophy of life, not merely a master of life by virtue of its moral order and discipline. She is indeed a supernatural organ of grace, the great sacrament of the life of God for souls. In touching souls through her sacramental functions, she remakes them, infusing them with a new life. All the Church's vital functions are for the sustenance and progress of this life. Thanks to this supernatural infusion, human life is elevated to the divine level and enters into the order which God desires for it. Its power of action and its influence then reach the plentitude God wishes them to have. It is not a mutilated life, active in the natural order, passive in the supernatural. Rather, it is a sanctified human life, one having the power of action which Divine Goodness has communicated to it. Civil society, without ceasing to be a natural form of life with its own ends as such, becomes supernaturalized in its own manner through the supernatural vivification of its members. We can say that the divine fragrance of the latter seeps into society, so that it is penetrated by this heavenly aroma, as soft linen may be permeated by the sweet odor of spikenard or roses. Men who are generously zealous for the Christian life and who are sanctified by grace, faith, and morality have the glowing light of Christ within them. And it is Jesus Himself who reappears and is secretly at work in His mystical members as they sincerely and earnestly accept His life.

When the number of these living members of Jesus Christ in civil society is increased, without society as such being the subject of divine life or incorporated as a member of the Church, it still remains touched, penetrated, and filled with this divine life which the sacraments spread among the individual members who live as children of God. The more extensive the sphere which these members of the Church occupy in the social ambit and, above all, the more profound and powerful their Christian life, the more the latter will penetrate society and the more firmly rooted in the divine order society and its directive organs will be. How could God's blessings fail to come down upon a nation whose life is ordered in this way? Peace becomes more firmly established, the collective conscience more healthy, social movements towards the common good more tranquil and expeditious, the exercise of authority more active and fruitful, submission to its direction easier and more docile, the natural abilities of man better employed, and the seeds of civilization within man able to find richer and more fertile fields.

In a civil society, weakness, failure, and crimes are inevitable. The sad heritage of corruption in all of us is so powerful that in some it is manifested spontaneously in the form of repugnant moral deformities. Oftentimes these moral wounds are not limited to a few isolated cases. There are public weakness which spread like a contagion through the social body. Worldly standards incompatible with the Gospel are joyously accepted by the multitudes, as if they were drinking a sweet poison without thinking what it is. Civil authority can do much to stop or lessen such epidemics. Yet it is not always within the power of civil authority to eliminate them if the co-operation of society is lacking. In such cases society lives more or less culpably in an environment of sin which cries to heaven, as do all transgressions of the moral law. Now it is an immense boon for this society to have many fervent Christians in whom the life of the Church is firmly rooted. These Christians are the divine counterbalance of human corruption and the active grain of salt which the hand of Providence sprinkles over sinful mankind, that it may not sink further into mortal disease. They are like an efficacious prayer for all, the expiatory victim for the sins of the many. Thanks to them, what would have been a disastrous torrent of avenging justice for the scorning of divine rights is often transformed into streams of mercy.

In this way the life and spirit of the Church deeply penetrate the collective conscience and the most hidden depths of society. It is a blessing of God that this supernatural life penetrates the inner core of society, for it makes possible moral health and order, well-being and integral progress. It is indeed a terrible misfortune that societies separate themselves from this holy influence which betters them and opens to them abundant sources of blessings. For when it is cut off from society, society gives free reign to the cancer of naturalism; and this gradually consumes all the living tissues of the social organism. It is a simple case of fatal blindness when leaders of peoples make it their task to extirpate the life of the Church and willfully separate men from the vivifying spirit of the Holy Mother of souls. Added to the frightful evil caused by this wayward procedure is the horrible sin these leaders commit in denying God the tribute of submission they owe Him by accepting the divine gift of the Church.

May God have mercy on nations which are proud of their oppression of the Holy Spouse of Jesus Christ, or which glory in eradicating her holy influence from society and seek to sever the relationship of creatures with the sovereign Master of all that exists.

Part II

THE CHURCH'S RELATIONSHIP
WITH THE INVISIBLE WORLD

Part II

Chapter I

THE CHURCH AND THE INVISIBLE WORLD

THERE is no visible creature which in some way does not have a relationship with the Church, that is, with the supernatural order established in society through Jesus Christ. Yet, since the Church does not end with time, she must have a unique relationship with the invisible world of eternity. All of God's creatures, by virtue of the fact that they are elements in a plan of most profound unity which links them all, must have — whether we know it or not — bonds of solidarity and close relationships among themselves. Because of the Church's being, dignity, and destiny, she must occupy a most important position among creatures and she must be the subject of relations which are not to be found in the other lower works. In this part of the book we shall consider the Church's relations with the invisible world. We shall begin in this chapter with those that link the Church with the blessed in heaven and with the angels.

I

We have already shown in our earlier volume of this series that the vital solidarity of the Church embraces purgatory and heaven and that there is very active communication between the Church on earth and these two invisible regions of the

Church triumphant.[1] Hence we shall have to add very little here concerning the relations between the visible supernatural society in this world and that of the holy souls in purgatory and the blessed in heaven.

The Church on earth is a living organism for the formation of saints. This is her great task in the world, and all her vital functions point to it. Yet the Church is not an instrument for effects and divine works which spring from her in the sense that works of human industry are produced in factories. Nor is she like a tree whose fruits are picked for man's needs. No, the Church is a tree whose fruits, already ripe for heaven, do not remain always in the same place on the tree, yet never disappear or are plucked. Christians who die in the peace of the Lord always remain in the transcendent being of the Church as her immortal members and as active organs of invisible action on behalf of the members still being formed here in the world. If a Christian who dies in the state of grace has his accounts with Divine Justice settled, his soul, pure and radiant, instantly enters into the enjoyment of the beatific vision. His intellect, having become like a wondrous light, and his will, burning with love, penetrate with ineffable delight the deep abyss of God's life in order to remain there for eternity with marvelous vigor and energy, in an existence serene and peaceful beyond our power to conceive. If the soul in grace leaves this world with what is called the legacy of sin — that is, its debt to Divine Justice — it must, before it can submerge itself in this deep mystery of glory, be freed from the harsh bonds which separate it from the glorious embrace of God. Yet, whether in purgatory or heaven, all these holy souls are living organs of the Church triumphant

---

[1]*The Catholic Church: The Mystical Body of Christ*, pp. 142-156.

and powers that are prodigiously beneficial for souls that are still forming themselves in Christ for eternity.

The Church constantly increases the number of these active invisible members as she sends numbers of her children from her motherly embrace to the arms of her Bridegroom and to the bosom of the heavenly Father. Each holy soul that enters purgatory is a gift to the Church of heaven from the Church on earth and a triumph of the sacrifice of Jesus in the human family through the Church. Each time a totally purified soul ascends amid splendor from purgatory to heaven, it becomes an eternal rose of light and of love which the Heavenly Gardener causes to glow in glory, after having lovingly cultivated it on earth and brought it to the purifying state of purgatory. Considered in this way, the Church is a river which continually sends forth its fragrant waters into the sea of the beatific vision. While her children have been forming themselves in Jesus Christ in this world, the Church has given them inexpressible care and tenderness till at last she has brought them, living in God, through the fearful ordeal of death (unless, as in some cases, it is at that very moment that she has had the happiness of gaining them completely for her heavenly Bridegroom).

When she places the souls of her children in purgatory, she never forgets them nor does she leave them without assuring them first of the glorious peace of heaven. Every day at Mass and at the end of each canonical hour, the Holy Spouse of Jesus casts a loving glance at the souls of her beloved children in purgatory. She sends forth a confident prayer to her omnipotent Bridegroom on behalf of these holy fruits of both of their lives. Yet our good Mother the Church is not content with this alone. She has at her command the infinite merits of Jesus, of the Blessed Virgin and of the saints. She can place her hand on these riches, with their expiatory value, and then apply them, in the form of indulgences gained by the faithful, for the benefit of the souls in purgatory. As a dew of grace these aids then fall on the holy region of pain with the peace of charity. The Church, with her prayers and the invaluable action of the Holy Sacrifice of the Mass, unceasingly liberates souls, souls that then pass from the patient love of purgatory to the glorious love of heaven. After having formed these souls in Christ crucified in this life, the Church with divine assiduity beneficently employs herself for their liberation from the expiatory pains of the next world.

The current of charity which ascends from earth to purgatory is not a message which remains unanswered. It finds its response in the increasing love of the holy souls for God and for the interests of Jesus Christ in the world. Although incapable of helping themselves except by expiatory suffering, they can move the heart of the heavenly Father in our behalf. They love God with an ardent, generous and pure love. In them there is no trace of egotism, no human meanness to contaminate their acts. They are holy and humble, pure and generous; they are entirely united to the holy will of God; they are most eager to pay with pain their debt to the justice of the Lord. And they know how to pray. What will be the prayer of souls so submissive to the divine will in the midst of inconceivable suffering? How humble, how confident and penetrating will be their prayer for the Church in this world and for her members amid the hardships and dangers of life? When the poor woman who had suffered from hemorrhage confidently touched the hem of Jesus' garment, she regained her health. The cry of the Canaanite woman, which was more powerful than Jesus' apparent disdain, was sufficient to free the woman's daughter from the power of the devil. The noble and deep faith of the centurion gave back the infirm servant his health. In like manner, the holy, humble cries full of unshakable faith in divine mercy on the part of the souls in purgatory are changed, in passing through the heart of God, into a perfumed breeze of graces which scatters its aroma and encourages those still in the field of battle.

Beyond purgatory is heaven, the happy home of those children of God who have carried to its final end their life in Jesus Christ. Heaven is the abode of truth and of satiating and beatific love. Pain, weeping, and fear have no place there. Those bitter trials of spiritual purification and those painful actions by which the Lord forms souls will have passed. In heaven there is no trace of fault or pain; souls are perfect in Christ and are gloriously united to Him. They are only waiting the last touch of glory at the resurrection of their bodies. Now they are living rays of light absorbed in the eternal sun whence all light comes. The Church has a living faith in these her glorious members and she invokes them in her continuous urgent needs. She knows that they do not scorn her; she knows that they listen to her cries. Among the blessed are the saints she has raised to the honors of the altar. They are the most outstanding souls formed in the heart of their Mother; they have left their vivid memory in the heart of the Church and in incontestable proofs of their heroic sanctity. The holy Spouse of Jesus enjoys contemplating these her eminent children, the pride of her life, and the authentic testimony of her holiness and her action on souls. She reminds the faithful that they should imitate the virtues of the saints. The Church praises these glorious children of hers and asks them to use their power before the Lord, that He may rescue her from danger, that she may spread her grace among men, and that those who are beginning their formation in Jesus may persevere to the end. The confident prayer of the Church is indefatigable. Every day she recalls to the memory of the faithful the illustrious example of the saints; every day she renews the Eucharistic sacrifice for the glory of God, including in it the remembrance of her children in heaven. These ardent prayers reach heaven as was witnessed by the prophet who saw them rise like fragrant incense through the hands of angels in the presence of the Lord.[2]

The cries of the Church are not lost in a vacuum, nor does their echo fail to reach souls in glory. These rejoice in this tribute from the holy Spouse of Jesus Christ. They also rejoice in the Church's effort to obtain, through them, from omnipotent Love the many different graces sought for her and needed for remedying innumerable evils. Above all, the Church needs these graces for her most important task, the one towards which her whole life is directed — that of forming souls in Jesus Christ. A fragrant aroma of prayers and the sweet voice of praise rise from the earth and are disseminated throughout heaven among the happy inhabitants of the heavenly homeland, those who so greatly love the Church. And in return, a shower of divine flowers, a heavy dew of blessings, mysterious radiations of life, come from heaven to fortify, alleviate, and console the Church in her struggles and prayer. All the saints of heaven participate in this work, although there are certain preferences among them. They either seek a gift of God on behalf of some need on earth, or for the benefit of certain souls, communities or nations which seem to be placed under the special protection of one of these blessed friends of God. Such a division of work in heaven does not exist because of penury or limited power of the glorious members of the Church. Rather, it exists because of the beneficent providence of God, who thus better attracts our failing attention and embraces us, through a thousand living organs, with His merciful love, whence all blessings come.

---

[2] Cf. Apoc. 8:3-4.

There is, then, a closely knit network of mutual influences between the Church on earth and that in heaven. The threads of which it is woven like an intangible veil of light are as numerous as the blessed in heaven. There is not one of these blessed to whom the Church on earth is indifferent, not one who does not contribute his thread to the very fine web of mercies which covers the entire being of the Church militant like an immense canopy made up of intercessions. There are no foolish dreams, no impotent aspirations, in this mysterious communication between heaven and earth, but rather a very vital reality and an incessant ebb and flow of graces between the two worlds in which the children of God are living.

Among these influxes which, like a loving glance of mercy, descend from heaven through each saint, we wish to call attention to one especially. Leaving out the sublime influence of the Blessed Virgin, since she is above all the saints and hence not here considered as one of them, we refer to those spiritual favors which come to us through the patriarch Saint Joseph.

Chosen by God to be the spouse of the Virgin and to act as the father of Jesus in this world, the holy patriarch has been so close, in a way no one else has, to the great mystery of the Incarnation as to remain enveloped in its dazzling splendors. After the Blessed Virgin, one cannot conceive of a soul holier and more filled with God. And after the influence of his spouse there is no other influence in the Church so widespread and universal as that of Saint Joseph. He who was the father of Jesus here on earth can indeed be the Patron of the universal Church, which is the same Jesus mystically diffused in His members. The holy patriarch did not give Jesus His human life. Yet he was the one who looked after it and who experienced an ineffable joy and sublime dignity in that his work and sweat earned the bread which Jesus ate. Such an intimate

and privileged service in behalf of Jesus demanded that Saint
Joseph should continue it in heaven in reference to the Mystical Body of the Redeemer. This is the reason for his universal patronage. That venerable face which so often looked
into the eyes of Jesus in Bethlehem, in the desert, in Egypt,
and in Nazareth; those eyes which so often rested upon the
sacred humanity of Him who called him father, are the face
and eyes which now, in a movement of prayer, seek out the
Church in the great splendor of light of the blessed. And
just as Jesus' glance never failed to find that of His earthly
father, in whom He always found generous love and a purity
worthy of the Blessed Virgin and of the Word made flesh,
so now the gaze of the Church towards her universal Protector never fails to find in him help in the trials of this life
and the fulfillment of life's needs.

The Church does not walk through this valley of tears
without holy companionship and powerful invisible assistance.
The life of God poured forth into so many living organs, such
as the blessed in heaven and the souls in purgatory, is changed
into an immense starry sky, as it were, which covers the Church.
In this sky each star is a holy soul praying for the Spouse of
Jesus Christ and continually sending over the skies the ray
of its intercessory light.

II

It pleased God to create, besides the material world, another world, one of pure spirits: the angels. Their number
is prodigious; their variety, marvelous. The creation that is
perceived through the senses is but a feeble sketch of the
splendor, riches, and power of this spiritual world. As a work
of intelligence and love it could not be lacking in excellent
order. We do not know much about it. Yet, by investigating
what is found in revelation concerning the angels, the human

mind has been able to form the body of angelical theology. Theologians who hold the Incarnation as the guiding principle and end of all divine works are compelled to bring in the idea of Jesus Christ in the creation of the angels. God had to create them looking at His Son made man. The angels thus are born of creative Love and penetrated by the pure splendor of Jesus Christ, as if the natural and supernatural beauty of Jesus were reflected in their spiritual nature, which Love also raised to the supernatural order. The innumerable multitude of angels can be reduced to three hierarchical orders, divided into nine choirs, three in each hierarchy. We could say that the choir is the harmonious concert of innumerable spirits, and the hierarchy the orderly grouping of the choirs in the scale of excellence.

It would seem that each choir is a reflection, in the natural order, of a divine attribute which reason sees in God. Each angel is an idea of the attribute reflected in its choir and made concrete in an individual spiritual nature that is both active and powerful. It has been placed in creation by God to show the divine attribute He has desired to manifest by it. The angel, knowing his own being and subjecting himself to God's sovereignty, is a living commendation of the attribute he reflects. Reflections of Divine Goodness or of the unreserved love of God thus ascend from the celestial hierarchy — that is, from the nine angelic choirs ranging from angels to seraphim — those burning coals of love in whom is manifested the powerful and active existence of Him whom Saint John defined as love: "God is Love."[3] All of this powerful world, so mysterious to us, is connected with Jesus Christ. Looking upon Jesus it was created, and waiting upon Jesus

---

[3] I John 4:16.

it was sanctified. The angels were called, in Jesus, to the dignity of children of God. Their powerful natural being, keen and vigorous, received the infusion of the divine life. A new light shone in their profound and active intellects. It was the light of revelation, which showed them the order to which they were elevated, for it was not by nature knowable to them. Also manifested to them were the delicate relationships which, through this elevation, they contracted with the Divine Persons and with the Sacred Humanity, through whom they received the gift. The clear and lofty idea of Jesus had to flash like lightning in the brilliant angelic mind. In the Epistle to the Hebrews we read: "And again, when He brings the firstborn into the world, He says 'And let all the angels of God adore Him.' "[4] At the moment of their creation and elevation, the light of Christ's dignity shone for the angels. Jesus must have been to them, as is held by the doctrine we accept concerning the motive for the Incarnation, the test of faith, the noble proof to which the sovereign God subjected those sublime creatures.

Sacred Scripture tells us that there were faithful and rebellious angels.[5] With their trial some angels were established in the divine life; others lost it by refusing to be subject to God. Our poor reason cannot form an exact idea of that formidable act by which the angels exercised the total power of their being by accepting or rejecting the divine condition of their glory. Their keen, comprehensive and vigorous intellect had to focus its energy on that act alone. Their will, powerful and robust as was their intellect, had to accept or reject unwaveringly and willingly the divine will as manifested in Jesus, whom the angels had to adore. A cry of submissive adoration and of jubilant praise resounded in heaven as the

---

[4]Heb. 1:6.   [5]Cf. II Peter 2:4.

faithful angels humbly adored. Rebellious pride thundered across the heavens in the form of sacrilegious blasphemy as the proud angels rejected the divine sovereignty shown in Jesus Christ. From that moment the angelic world was divided into two groups. The proud angels possess inconceivable power and wondrous strength; forever irreconcilable, they are engaged in obstinate struggle in the field where they attempt to exert their power in the service of their profound malice.

The good angels, confirmed in grace, received the brilliant light of glory which was transformed into eternal happiness. From the moment of their test they were and will always be creatures eternally in possession of the glorious divine life. Jesus, the source of this life for every creature, was from that moment their head; in hope before the Incarnation, in reality after it. The good angels are, rightfully, living members of this Mystical Body vivified by the spirit of Jesus, the Church in eternity. They are not nor can they be members of the visible Church on earth. Yet they are members of the Church in her integral transcendent being, which, prevailing over time and the changeable forms of earthly life, will be forever the glorious Mystical Body of the Divine Head, Jesus Christ. Between the Church in time and that of eternity, therefore, in which angels are present like spiritual flowers in living garlands of the light of glory, there must necessarily be an intimate and vital relationship, which will bring about active communication between the angels and the Church on earth.

The existence of this communication is beyond the shadow of a doubt. The infallible word of God has given us thousands of testimonies concerning it before and after Jesus Christ's appearance in the world. The angels came as friends of Abraham,[6] they saved Lot from the destruction of Sodom,[7]

6Cf. Gen. 18:2ff.   7Cf. Gen. 19:15-17.

they appeared to Jacob in a mysterious dream through which
he received the consolation of God,[8] they went before the
people of God in the miraculous column of smoke and fire
which guided them through the desert,[9] they invisibly fought
against the enemies of God's people,[10] and often they inter-
vened on behalf of these chosen people.[11] In Babylon they
closed the lions' mouth in order that the lions might not devour Daniel,[12] they brought him food through Habacuc, who
was carried by an angel from Judea to Babylon,[13] and in
Helidorus they avenged the profaning of the holy temple of
the Lord.[14] The entire history of the chosen people is a brilliant testimony of the beneficent and provident power of angels
on behalf of men in that forerunner of the Church, a pro-
logue as it were of the true Church of Jesus Christ.

Was the angels' intervention less real or powerful after
the coming of Christ and the founding of the Church on
earth? No, it was not. The angel Gabriel prepared Zachary's
soul for the great event of the coming of the Desired One
of Israel, for whom Zachary's own son had to prepare the
hearts of his people.[15] It was the angel Gabriel again who
announced to the Blessed Virgin the mysterious plan by which
she was to become the Mother of Jesus.[16] An angel of the
Lord, perhaps the same one, soothed Saint Joseph in his painful
doubts and revealed to him the ineffable mystery which had
taken place in his spouse.[17] An angel announced to the shep-
herds at Bethlehem the birth of Jesus, and angels sang the
"Gloria in excelsis Deo" on that memorable night.[18] Angels

---

[8]Cf. Gen. 28:12.
[9]Cf. Exodus 13:20-21; 14:19.
[10]Cf. Judg. 6:12ff.
[11]Cf. 4 Kings 19:35.
[12]Cf. Dan. 6:22.
[13]Cf. Dan. 14:33-36.

[14]II Mach. 3:4-26.
[15]Cf. Luke 1:11-21.
[16]Cf. Luke 1:26-38.
[17]Cf. Matt. 1:20-21.
[18]Cf. Luke 2:9:15.

took care to deliver Jesus from the wrath of Herod,[19] and an angel advised Saint Joseph to return to Galilee from Egypt.[20] Angels served Jesus after His fast in the desert,[21] and one comforted Him in the tremendous agony in Gethsemani.[22] An angel announced the resurrection of the Lord to the holy women at dawn on the first day of the week.[23]

After Jesus had ascended into heaven, the angels carefully took care of the budding Church. They began at the very hour of the Ascension. As the eyes and hearts of the disciples were captivated by the beloved Master who was ascending through the clouds heavenwards, two angels told the disciples to return to Jerusalem and to await the coming of the Holy Spirit promised by Jesus.[24] An angel liberated the apostles who were put in prison by the Sanhedrin,[25] another appeared to the deacon Philip,[26] and still another to the centurion Cornelius.[27] An angel rescued the Prince of the apostles from Herod and from "all that the Jewish people were expecting."[28] We find these and many more facts in the same inspired books. Therefore, during the long course of the centuries in which the Church has been on earth, there have been given frequent and irrefutable testimonies showing that the angels never leave the Spouse of Jesus Christ.

We know that God has given each soul into the care of a guardian angel[29] and that the Church affectionately celebrates a feast of the holy guardian angels. We know that these invisible friends of souls never leave their charges until they have seen the divine plan completed in them, or until souls obstinately tear themselves away from the merciful Love which

---

19Cf. Matt. 2:13.
20Cf. Matt. 2:19-20.
21Cf. Matt. 4:11.
22Cf. Luke 22:43.
23Cf. Mark 16:2-8.
24Cf. Acts 1:10-11.

25Cf. Acts 5:19-20.
26Acts 8:26.
27Cf. Acts 10:3-7.
28Cf. Acts 12:7-11.
29Cf. Matt. 18:10.

pursues them even to the hour of death. We also know that besides the angels for individual souls there are angels for nations, the particular churches, religious orders, and the universal Church. Saint Michael is the glorious spirit who in the name of God protects and guards the holy Spouse of Jesus Christ. We know that through the ministry of angels the Lord has accomplished stupendous marvels in His servants on earth. A crucified seraphim imprinted the sacred wounds on Saint Francis of Assisi with bloody rays of light. As Blessed Lydwina lay sick on her poor bed, her guardian angel is said to have told her of the needs of the whole world, that she might employ the power of her prayer and the pains of her sacrificed life to fulfill them. A small angel with a face of flame pierced the heart of Saint Theresa of Avila with a golden dart as she knelt rapt in ecstasy. The lives of the saints are full of interventions which testify to the certain existence of these angelic spirits. Reason aided by faith realizes that for each of these known manifestations there are innumerable others hidden from our human experience, yet real in the lives of the children of God, now one at a time, now united in groups or moral persons in the unity of the Church.

The minute and hidden action of many microscopic organisms in the heart of nature is intensive, extensive, and continual. The discoveries of science on this point have gradually allowed us to penetrate this enchanted world, so prodigiously small that its activity could hardly be suspected. This life which develops in plants and animals, these diminutive beings which are so wonderfully multiplied and which our eyes cannot see, are tributary to our own organic life. The spiritual life of the children of God, the vast and fertile field of the Church, is no less vitalized by the invisible influence of the angels. How wonderful it would be if with eyes capable of seeing the mystery of what is by nature invisible to us, we

could view the myriads of angels who work for our formation in Jesus Christ without ceasing to contemplate the face
of the heavenly Father! What dazzling brilliance would en-
velop us if, tearing aside the veil of mystery, our soul could
see the admirable angelic world submerged in the light of
God and occupied in behalf of our sanctification. Saint Frances
of Rome was amazed at seeing spring forth from the creative
act of God such a great multitude of angels that even the
thick snowflakes in a heavy snowfall could not be compared
to their number. All these manifestations of light, bathed in
the divine splendors, work for us in the heart of the Church.
The Church itself is enveloped in the invisible yet dazzling
nimbus of angels. Blessed Angela of Foligno in visions saw
the angels around our tabernacles like a swarm of bees from
heaven drawing nectar from the Eucharistic rose of Jesus in
the Blessed Sacrament. More rapidly than the rays of the
sun travel, the angels respond to the urgent call of a soul that
prays. Joyfully and reverently they gather the prayers of the
holy, as if they were grains of fragrant incense, and offer
them in golden censers before the altar of eternity.

The Church firmly believes in the angelic life and in the
continual action of the angels in the children of God. Each
day, in the Preface of the Mass, she remembers these heavenly
inhabitants who, through Jesus, praise the most holy Trinity
with their eternal hymn of glory. Each day she remembers
in her "Te Deum" the holy canticle of the angelic choirs.
The life of the angels seems to be fused with that of the
Church on earth, as if beneath this visible place of struggle
and combat there was spread a fine net of gold, with which
the angels gather for heaven, as immortal flowers, the holy
souls who, when they leave this life, are carried, as the Church
says in her liturgy, by the angels to the bosom of God.

One night, as the holy patriarch Jacob wearily walked on his journey from Mesopotamia, he stopped to sleep in a field under the open sky. A marvelous dream unexpectedly awakened him. At the place where he rested his head there was a mysterious ladder reaching to heaven. A dazzling line of angels ascended the ladder to heaven and another descended from heaven to earth. The Lord stood beside Jacob and spoke to him. On hearing the voice of the Lord, who renewed the promises made to his fathers, Jacob fearfully exclaimed: "How awesome is this place! This is none other than the house of God; this is the gate of heaven."[30] The Church always has these resplendent legions of angels, rising to heaven laden with the rich harvest of holy works performed in the Church and descending from heaven bearing the blessings of God, which in an invisible manner they bestow on men. "Holy is this place," we could say on seeing the Church extended over the world; certainly she is the house of God and the gate of heaven. Although many Christians have failed to observe this consoling truth which invisibly operates for our formation as children of God, the Church herself knows and recognizes its reality. And the Church believes in and praises God through the holy angels who are continually occupied in helping her in her divine work of generating and rearing the innumerable children of God who are formed in her.

III

There is in this beneficent influence of the good angels over the Church an interesting aspect which we must mention in completing our explanation of the relationship of the Church to the angelic world. It is the help which the holy angels give to the Church and her members in their struggles with Satan.

---

[30]Cf. Gen. 28:11-17.

The rebellious angels have not been confined to hell without power to intervene in the world. By permission of the holy and wise providence of God, the demons are able to tempt and to test men in a thousand ways. Our diabolical enemies have made more than a little use of this permission. Their sin, stripping them of grace and closing the doors of heaven to them forever, has not destroyed their powerful nature. Their natural powers are intact and vigorous, but are now at the service of cultivated malice and inextinguishable hatred. The fallen angels do not and cannot love one another. They do not submit their will to legitimate authority. Rather, they keep themselves in the inexorable hierarchy of their being imposed on them by violence. In this union of common hate and persistency in evil, they attack the world with the malicious intention of snatching souls from Jesus Christ, for they know they can do nothing else against omnipotent and merciful Love. In their own way they mock the providence of God in the good angels. The demons prowl about the world to tempt men. From time to time we may have to suffer the cunning attacks of these powerful enemies. There are demons for every type of sin and for the irritation of every passion. There is a devil for every interest of hell. Who could enumerate the variety of tricks which they employ with indefatigable malice, a malice which is applied and sustained with a hatred that never dies? Who could count the number of these invisible perpetrators of iniquity whom Lucifer sends into the world for the destruction of souls? These are not vain fantasies nor the cowardly deliriums of tepid souls. The infallible word of God shows us the informal enemy as a roaring lion, going about seeking someone to devour.[31] Often many are concentrated at one place, as in that unfortunate town of

---

[31]Cf. I Peter 5:8-9.

Gerasa. When Jesus asked the Gerasene man possessed by
the devil what his name was, he answered "Legion," for
many devils had entered into him.[32] Often the demons line
up like an invisible army which overruns everything.[33] Their
action is very powerful, though it has not the force to destroy
man's liberty. With the Lord's permission, they can fill the
human body with hideous leprosy as they did with holy Job,
after ruining his property and causing the death of his children.[34] Within the twinkling of an eye, they can transport a
person from one place to another. This terrible power was
experienced by Jesus Himself in His sacred humanity.[35] With
God's permission they can bring about tempests, move the
elements with a resounding clamor, disturb the imagination,
arouse the passions, stimulate the appetites of the flesh. Their
power is extensive, great, and penetrating. Would they re-
frain from using it among men, since they can introduce their
diabolical action into human life? No, they would not. They
intervene, then, in man's life with obstinate constancy and
with an incalculable variety of stratagems which would fill
us with horror if we could see them. They work in the
imagination, in the appetites, in organic powers. They operate
among the multitudes, where they know how to use the power
of suggestion for evil purposes. They exploit, in an amazing
way, human weaknesses, mass psychology, and predominant
naturalistic ideas. They know how to conceal themselves when
they are tempting man, how to dissimulate their intentions,
and to cloak their evil designs with the appearance of good
or specious desirability. These demons attentively watch the
stirrings of the human heart, and they go along with the
tastes of each man. If the actions of the angels are incalcul-

---

[32]Cf. Luke 8:26-33.
[33]Cf. Eph. 6:12.

[34]Cf. Job 1:13-22; 2:1-8.
[35]Cf. Matt. 4:5-8.

able because of their extent and variety, also incalculable is the cunning action of devils, which is even more extensive and varied than we can suspect. If we could see, from backstage, the spiritual drama of life, we would be amazed at the forces which secretly battle against and stir, without, however, any detriment to their freedom, the characters on the visible stage of life. We are not like putty in their hands, since we have not lost control of our actions. Yet with our unrestrained passions and desires we sometimes serve designs very different from those we think we are seeking and fulfilling in this life.

Now this tenacious and obstinate action of the spirit of evil upon man and against the Church is a hidden struggle against the powers of darkness who were denounced by St. Paul.[36] It is this action which the holy angels continually ward off, in order to protect the children of God. Frequently there appear in the Church, like the buds of a rosebush, enterprises for the glory of God and the good of souls, generous intentions promising abundant spiritual fruits. Ordinarily, formidable storms are unleashed against such intentions and undertakings. Is it only the opposition of human egotism, the warped viewpoint, envy and jealousy of men that threaten and interevene in this tempest? No, such is not the case. In the invisible world there are formidable diabolical powers engaged in this combat which cause the human elements to appear to be the subject of altercation. The Church is constantly attacked by these invisible armies which, though they cannot destroy her, passionately take possession of those of her members who do not know how to resist the enemy firmly by remaining steadfast in the faith and docilely submitting themselves to the authority of the Church.

36Cf. Eph. 6:12.

Saint Michael and his angels waged war against these invisible armies of demons.[37] The tremendous battle in heaven which resulted in the ejection of Lucifer and his followers from that place,[38] continues to rage throughout the course of the Church's existence because of the demon's attacks. Each peril avoided by the Spouse of Jesus Christ is an episode in the battle of the centuries; each schism or heresy, every moment of apostasy among nations, is a tremendous laceration of the Mystical Body produced by the fatal genius of evil. In the first rebellion in the angelic world, a great multitude of spirits denied the divine authority. In the rebellion against God and the Church which the demons of hell provoke among men, these evil spirits drag many children of God from the Church and raise gigantic obstacles — thus impeding many souls who otherwise would have attained truth, from entering the city of God.

This fearful struggle will cease only at the end of the world. Invisibly present among us, these two powerful armies wage war, fighting over us as if for a coveted prize. It is because of the defense of the good angels that the demons do not cause more havoc in the world. We can never acknowledge sufficiently what the good angels do for us in this titanic struggle. Saint Paul tells us that "the mystery of iniquity is already at work."[39] It does not advance with all its violent and destructive power because a mysterious obstacle checks it.[40] A day will arrive in which this obstacle will recede a little, not because of weakness or fatigue, but that the plan of God may be fulfilled.[41] Then the ravages wrought by the diabolical anti-Christ will be astounding.[42] But another day will come in which the triumphant power and the formidable dominion

---

37 Apoc. 12:7-12.
38 Apoc. 12:9.
39 II Thess. 2:7.

40 Cf. II Thess. 2:6.
41 Cf. II Thess. 2:8.
42 Cf. II Thess. 2:9-11.

of evil will be reduced to powerlessness by the breath of the Lord Jesus.[43] What is this force which rises like a concrete wall to block the tremendous onslaught of anti-Christ in the world? A learned commentator on Saint Paul, Father Prat, sees in this hidden power the peerless archangel Saint Michael, the angel of the universal Church, who will ward off the violent forces of Satan's army.[44]

The Church confidently invokes the holy angels, and she has a particular devotion to their prince, Saint Michael, who in the fierce combat knows how to repel Lucifer with the triumphant cry: "May the Lord rebuke thee."[45] In her struggle against the spirit of darkness, the Church knows that she is not alone or unarmed. Jesus has given her the power to check the devil with holy means which she freely uses. They are the sacraments and sacramentals.[46] Jesus has also given us, as an impenetrable breastplate, the noble army of the good angels under the command of Saint Michael, who invisibly protects and defends the Church.

We have thus briefly explained the very active relationship of the Church on earth with the invisible Church of eternity and the gloomy world of hell, which seeks the annihilation of the Church. Although Satan plucks, like so many dry leaves, thousands of bad Christians from the holy tree of the Church, his own diabolical assaults serve to make secure in Jesus Christ and to prosper in Him that society against which the powers of hell shall never prevail.

---

[43]Cf. II Thess. 2:8.

[44]Prat, Ferdinand, S. J., *La Théologie de Saint Paul,* 8th ed., Vol. I, pp. 98-99. This work has been published in English translation by Burns Oates and Washbourne under the title *The Theology of St. Paul.*

[45]Jude 9.

[46]Cf. Mark 16:17.

Chapter II

THE CHURCH AND THE BLESSED VIRGIN

AMONG the relationships of the Church with the invisible world there is one especially which is superior to those we have thus far mentioned; so important is it that it is lower than and subject to only those relationships the Church has with Jesus, the heavenly Father, and the Holy Spirit. This relationship is the one which exists between the Church and the Blessed Virgin. The subject is indeed extensive, yet we shall try to treat it under three points in this chapter.

What is the Blessed Virgin in relation to the Church? She is the model, the Mother, and the heart of the Church.

I

The Blessed Virgin was chosen to be the Mother of Jesus. She was associated with the whole work of redemption and sanctification. Hence God gave her the highest dignity that can possibly be given to a pure creature, and He imparted to her the exact measure of grace which her eminent dignity and function demanded. As the Mother of God, the Blessed Virgin possessed a dignity which bordered on the infinite. She had to have, therefore, that plenitude of life and that penetration which wholly sanctified her being and which continually protected her against spiritual death. And as an associate of Jesus in His great work, she had to have fullness of communicative grace; that is, she had to possess it so as to diffuse it in creatures sanctified by Jesus. This extending of

96

life to others was not to result in diminution and damage to the Blessed Virgin's fullness of grace. For two reasons, then, God had to fill His Mother with grace and exempt her from the death of sin which every child of Adam contracts by natural generation. For these two reasons God also had to preserve her from birth from any trace of concupiscence and had to endow her with eminent gifts which would cause her life to grow without interruption till it reached that happy state that requires transition from earth to heaven. Poor human nature, though refined and most eminent in the Mother of God, would not be able to endure the violent force of love which was to reach its fullness in one who had always loved God supernaturally with all the strength of her being. The Blessed Virgin, because of her dignity and office, sought to be, and actually was, immaculate, full of grace, exempt from concupiscence, continually active in her ascent to God and crowned with the glorious resurrection of her body, which did not know sin and which was the living tabernacle and source of life for the Son of God. It was necessary that the Blessed Virgin, because of her eminent position as a being full of grace, should surrender herself voluntarily to God from birth and consecrate herself wholly and voluntarily to God from her birth, dedicating her entire being to Him; that is, she had to be a virgin in the full import of the word: a human creature forever consecrated to God in soul and body. At the proper time, when the Lord inspired her, she crowned this first and total consecration to God with a vow — it is evident that she was vowed to virginity, from the answer she gave to the angel when he announced the Incarnation to her. Full of grace, and with an intellect that was miraculously illumined, she gave herself wholly to God, and from that moment was a creature of honor and singular devotion, so totally consecrated to God as to be an inviolable deposit of the divine life of grace.

We do not know how much information concerning Jesus Christ God gave the Blessed Virgin at the first moment of her existence. He whom jubilant angels saluted the instant their powerful intellects opened to light — would He not perhaps be the brilliant central idea in which would be united the supernatural mysteries which God would show His Mother at the first moment of her existence as an intelligent creature? It seems to us that He would. This brilliant idea would undoubtedly penetrate that very clear intellect so miraculously moved by God. And from that moment it would gain possession of all the Blessed Virgin's powers, centering her whole life in the great future reality and directing it towards Him who chose her as His Mother, Him who was to be in a few years her Son. Although she might not know the mystery of her union with Jesus, she did know Jesus and the ministry He had come to discharge on earth. The Blessed Virgin adhered to Jesus as no other creature who knew and loved Him. And from the moment she knew Him there was no flame of love for Jesus in heaven and on earth more ardent and more powerful than that which was burning in her heart.

With the passing of the years, the Blessed Virgin came to know the magnitude of the design God had devised for her; namely, what she was to be to Jesus: a mother and a co-worker. Her burning love which caused her to be chosen as mother had to be extended to all creatures, and she had to have the keen desire of communicating to them the life which Jesus brought into the world for all those capable of receiving it. The divine maternity of the Blessed Virgin extends in a mysterious way from her Son to His mystical members. And the life which under the action of the Holy Spirit was powerful enough to give human life to Jesus, was made full enough and powerful enough to give divine life to Jesus' members. The divine maternity of the Blessed Virgin thus attained the fullness which God placed in Mary in making her His mother. She was the mother of the Mystical Body of Jesus, because she was the mother of the Divine Head of this Body.

Such are the characteristics which glow in the Blessed Virgin: the eminent dignity of Mother of God, fullness of grace with exemption from sin and concupiscence, untainted virginity, unfailing adherence to Jesus, and a limitless spiritual fruitfulness. She was chosen by God to be His mother; she lives in glory with Jesus as an associate in the sacred ministry of the Son of God made man and as one discharging, in this luminous height of creation elevated to the divine order, the function of diffusing the life of God or its reverberations to as many creatures as the Lord has placed under the command of Jesus Christ, creatures who do not obstinately resist His action.

Such is the eminent model of the Church. All the supernatural qualities which shine in the Church are in her brought to the most complete and eminent point to which the power of God can bring them.

In fact, the Church, as we are now considering her, the visible supernatural society of men with Jesus Christ, is, like the Blessed Virgin, associated with Jesus, full of grace, a virgin as is the Mother of Jesus, and the mother of all men who attain the dignity of sons of God.

Saint Paul tells us that Jesus: "also loved the Church, and delivered Himself up for her, that He might sanctify her, cleansing her in the bath of water by means of the Word; in order that He might present to Himself the Church in all her glory, not having spot or wrinkle."[1] Christian tradition has always regarded Holy Church as the associate of Jesus, born of Him, from His open side on the cross, in the same way that

---

[1]Eph. 5:25-27.

Eve was formed by God from Adam as the first man slept, that she might be his helpmate in all things.[2] From the very beginning the Church was chosen by Jesus Christ to be His Spouse and Mystical Body, intimately and vitally united to Him, the partaker of His sanctifying ministry and His inseparable companion. Next to the ineffable union and association of the Virgin with Jesus, one cannot conceive of a closer union or of a more intimate association than that of the Church with Jesus Christ.

This fusion of the Church with Jesus so that it is His visible organ for the sanctification of men required continual sanctity in this animated organ. Jesus gave this sanctity to the Church. He promised her His assistance until the consummation of the world and assured her that hell would never prevail against her.[3] The Church has been holy from her very first day as an organized society. The Holy Spirit triumphantly came upon the apostles at Pentecost, and from that time the Church has unerringly taught a pure doctrine of eternal life, has infallibly sanctified well-disposed souls, and securely guided all to their final end. The Church is not only holy in this her active and operative sanctity, but also in her very constitution and life, as we have thoroughly explained elsewhere.[4] Her soul is the Holy Spirit, who will never leave her unprotected or depart from her. In her social body there is always a prodigious number of souls in grace; and many — more than we can suspect — are saints, that is, heroically given to divine love and fully dominated by it. There has never been a moment in which the social body of the Church has not been holy. The Church has never experienced a moment of spiritual death, as we have until we received Baptism. She

[2]Cf. Gen. 2:18.
[3]Cf. Matt. 16:18.
[4]*The Catholic Church: The Mystical Body of Christ*, Part I, chapter i.

was born living in Christ. The sacrifice of the Redeemer was the price of the life and birth of His Spouse. From this divine sacrifice comes forth the wondrous effusion of the Spirit, which gives being and life to the admirable supernatural organism of the Church. The Spouse of Jesus Christ will never lose her sanctity. From her very beginnings she was confirmed in grace. The failures and infidelities of her children do not affect her substance. These fallen ones are like leaves which become dry through their own fault on the tree of eternal spring; they are like roses which of themselves wither on a rosebush of perennial verdure and untainted beauty.

The Church not only possesses perennial holiness, but progressive holiness, as we have explained in our earlier work, in speaking of her mystical growth.[5] The powers of holiness which she carries within her constantly develop and are unfailingly manifested, despite the failures of individuals. Yet the Church is so completely of Jesus in the entirety of her being that she belongs to no one except her Bridegroom, and there is no danger of her separating from Him or being unfaithful to Him. When a Christian consecrates himself to Jesus so that he belongs to Jesus alone and no one else possesses him, we say that he has made the vow of chastity. And if this chastity is intact, in that this body consecrated to Jesus has never been violated by carnal intercourse, it is virginal chastity. The Church is, in her order, always an inviolable virgin. She has never been anything but the possession of Jesus. She will perpetually be the Virgin Spouse of the Word made flesh.

Yet this untainted virginity is accompanied, as with the Blessed Virgin, by another admirable characteristic: fruitfulness. The Church, the virginal Spouse of Jesus, is the Mother of all the children of God in the world. Each baptized person is an effusion of the life of Jesus and a living reproduction of

---

[5]*The Catholic Church: The Mystical Body of Christ,* Part III, chapter v.

the Divine Spouse, a human creature who possesses the dignity of a child of God. Just as the Church's vital contact with Jesus and His complete possession of the Church make her a virgin, so her vital union with Him makes her a fruitful mother of all the children of God in the human family. And like a good mother, as she rears them she gives them her supernatural life and that of her Bridegroom. The Church possesses an eminent maternity. The more her children grow in the life she gives them, the more they are rooted in the heart of the Church. She is a mother who has always carried them in her arms as long as they are not culpably and brutally torn from her by some crime which separates them from her. What fruitfulness in the world can be compared to this divine fruitfulness? The centuries do not make the Church sterile, like an organism which declines because of senility. And the prototype of the Church in all this is she who is before the Church and above the Church, Virgin and Mother, the most holy and blessed Virgin.

The relations of the Virgin to the Church are such that one cannot view them as fortuitous or not intended by the Divine Artist who has made these two masterpieces for Jesus; namely, the Mother of Jesus and the Spouse of Jesus. The eminent characteristics of the mother are reflected in the Spouse: divine dignity, perennial holiness, continual and positive growth in grace, an immaculate state from the beginning, untainted virginity, and divine fruitfulness. The Christian mind and soul spontaneously associate these two admirable works of love and are pleased in looking at the Church to see it as the living mirror of the Blessed Virgin, and in considering the Blessed Virgin, to see her as the model and type of the Church. The Church lovingly gathers together the poetical expressions with which Scripture extols her, the holy Spouse of Jesus Christ; she weaves this fragrant garland of fresh roses into the Litany of Loreto and places it on the head of the Mother of God. What the Holy Spirit has sung about the mystical Spouse of Jesus Christ, the Church with sure instinct applies to and sings of the Blessed Virgin, as if the Divine Singer had directed such high praises to her before He sang them of the Church. It is not strange, then, that in the course of living tradition the Blessed Virgin and the Church have been uninterruptedly regarded as the new Eve. The Blessed Virgin is a counterbalance to Eve, who brought death; the Church is also a counterbalance because of her mysterious birth from the side of her Bridegroom asleep upon the cross. Each of them is, in her own order, the mother of the children of God.

II

This similarity between the Church and the Blessed Virgin is a close one. It is not fortuitous, but was intended and effected by God, who chose the Blessed Virgin for His Mother and His co-worker, and who formed the Church as the Spouse of Jesus and as Jesus' associate in His ministry of spiritual vivification among men. Yet this relationship is not the only one nor does it tell us all that the Blessed Virgin means to the Church. Besides being a model and exemplar, she is also the mother of the Church in a true spiritual sense.

The root of this maternity is the Blessed Virgin's motherhood in relation to Jesus Christ. Jesus is the Redeemer of mankind, the meritorious principle of the life which makes men children of God. Yet, in a mysterious way, He is at the same time the life and the Head of these members whom He supernaturally vivifies. The communication of the life of Jesus is not brought about by chance, but rather according to a plan that is well known and intended by Jesus. To each soul the Holy Spirit gives His singular gift of grace. Yet these individual and distinct gifts proceed from Jesus. Jesus knows them. And in order that they may operate in each soul within the organic unity of the Church, He has established His sacrifice as the principle of human rehabilitation and has made His sanctifying action the application of all redeeming merits. Jesus, then, is filled with gifts which are ready to be communicated. He is like a divine seed, full of vigor and power, which gradually causes to spring forth from itself — like renewals wisely directed — mystical members vivified by grace. The Church, an organism born of this vital expansion of Jesus, must necessarily be the mystical extension of Jesus Christ — His plenitude.[6]

Now the Son of God became flesh in the pure body of the Blessed Virgin with this purpose of communicating life to intelligent creatures, that is, with a redemptive intention toward mankind. And the Blessed Virgin, by her divine maternity, planted in the human family the vital seed which, once assimilated through faith and grace, would change it into the family of the children of God — that is, the Church. In the divine maternity of the Virgin there was embodied, then, this spiritual expansion of Jesus, which was known to and accepted by the Blessed Virgin when she gave her consent to the Incarnation. To be the mother of Jesus was equivalent to being the mother of the Mystical Body of Jesus at its root and vital principle. Although in the body of his mother a child is not formed in the fullness of his vigor and with the appearance of a mature man, even when he is fully developed the child does not cease to be the mother's, since from her he received his body, which was formed from and in hers with the inherent power of developing into what it later became. The mother, because of what she gives to the child, is his mother in what through natural growth comes later. In applying this truth to the divine order of communication of

---

[6]Cf. 1:23.

grace in Jesus Christ, the Blessed Virgin is properly the mother of the Mystical Body of Jesus, the Church, because she is the mother of Jesus Christ who is its germinal principle.

The truth of the previous considerations on the divine maternity of the Blessed Virgin appears clearer and more complete when linked with her office as a co-worker of Jesus in all His works.

Jesus wished the Blessed Virgin to be not only His mother but His associate in His universal ministry. He had to make her, therefore, a depository of His intentions, and He had to communicate to her His own sentiments regarding men and the supernatural elevation of all creation. The fidelity of the Blessed Virgin to her vocation did the rest. She united herself intimately to her Son in the exercise of His saving ministry and ordered, with power and stability, the whole course of her life in the direction in which Jesus channeled His. She desired, then, man's rehabilitation through the sacrifice of her Son. And as she consented to the Incarnation, she likewise consented fully to the redemption which was wrought through the painful immolation of Jesus. Thus she embraced fervently this sacrifice for herself and made of her own life an immolation which was to be associated and fused with the immensely painful immolation of her Son. If the sacrifice of Jesus, therefore, is, because of its end and its intrinsic efficacy, the redemption of mankind, the Blessed Virgin's sacrifice, made along with His, is also — in its order — a principle of the divine life which the redemption brings to men. The merits of the Blessed Virgin enter into the infinite current of the merits of her Son, like a transparent stream, not because Jesus needs them to complete His own, but because in His love He desired to associate the life of His Mother with His own life, in order that both, being fused as a sacrifice, might be the meritorious cause of our salvation.

We can follow the course of a river upstream until we reach its source. There we find the principle of that current of water which moves along over a wide stretch till it empties into the sea. When we reflect on the course of the life of grace, we arrive, guided by faith, at the sacred springs of life: the heart of Jesus, opened by a lance as He hung upon the cross, and the heart of Mary, in its compassion fused with that of her Son at the foot of the cross. Here was the cradle of the Church; there the abundant fount which brings life to the vast world of souls and also to the more vast invisible world of the angels. Jesus and Mary, united in a common painful sacrifice, are the meritorious principle of our life as children of God. Is it then strange that the Church and Christian souls, gazing upon the Virgin at the foot of the cross, should salute her with the sweet name of mother and esteem her as such?

Here it is necessary to make use of an illustration in order that we may better understand the mystery we are considering.

Because of the very nature of things, Jesus is not called the father of the Church, but her Head and Bridegroom. The Church is the spiritual fullness of Jesus, His vital extension in men and in angels. In the former, in order to establish itself as a visible, continuous social body on earth; in the latter and in souls already belonging to Jesus in eternity, in order to form the Church triumphant, definitive and eternal. Between the Church and Jesus there is a vital bond of immanence and compenetration, which cannot be removed or isolated without destroying the Church. Jesus' own concept of the Church is as His Mystical Body: Jesus in His integrity and in the plenitude of His mystical being. For this reason Jesus is not called the father of the Church, but rather her Head and Bridegroom, because the union between the Church and Jesus is for the formation of only one complete being — Christ, perfect and complete in the extension of His life among His members.

Here the Blessed Virgin's status as Mother of the Church appears most vigorous and brilliant: Just as through the Incarnation Mary belongs to Jesus, through co-operation in the vivifying sacrifice she is mother of what is truly born of that sacrifice. We see two very solemn moments of immense consequence in the life of the Virgin: (1) her consent to the Incarnation; (2) her consent to the redeeming death of Jesus. In the first she offers her life that she may become, through the action of the Holy Spirit, the Mother of Jesus; in the second, she offers the life of Jesus, loved a thousand times more than her own, that from this sacrifice the children of God may be born, or what amounts to the same, that Jesus might be extended in the mystical fullness of His being. Could one then deny the Blessed Virgin the title of Mother of the Church and of the children of God?

But in order that no trace of doubt might remain, about this, Jesus desired to proclaim Himself the mystery of the spiritual maternity which was taking place in His mother through the sacrifice of Calvary. Hence with His omnipotent word He brought to its consummation Mary's spiritual maternity.

Leaving His mother in the reverent care of Saint John just before He died, Jesus did not limit Himself to entrusting the Blessed Virgin to the filial solicitude of the beloved disciple. The word of Jesus was more profound and prodigiously filled with meaning. Saint John writes: "When Jesus, therefore, saw His mother and the disciple standing by, whom He loved, He said to His mother, 'Woman, behold thy son.' Then He said to the disciple, 'Behold thy mother.' "[7] Tradition does not see in these words only a pious charge of Jesus to the disciple on behalf of His mother. It has always seen in

---

[7] John 19:26-27.

them the intimate operation and the clear proclamation of the
spiritual maternity of the Blessed Virgin. If perhaps anything
remained to be done at this point that the Blessed Virgin might
truly be the spiritual mother of men, the omnipotent word of
Jesus on that occasion completed it. The mind, heart, and soul
of the Virgin had to be prodigiously expanded in accordance
with the irresistible power of the words of Jesus, in order to
conceive and bring to light, in that moment of inconceivable
love and immense pain, the vast offspring of Jesus crucified.
The Church began there and remained as conceived in the
soul of the Virgin. Days later, with the solemn coming of
the Holy Spirit, the Church would be manifested publicly as a
formed society, and she would begin to be diffused throughout
the world, never to cease in her extensive growth through the
conquest of souls and peoples, nor in her intensive development
through the continual expansion of her hidden powers. The
child, in growing to manhood, we have already said, does not
cease to be the son of his mother. The Church, always growing
till the end of time, never loses her status as the Mystical
Body of Jesus Christ or as the supernatural society of souls
which began on the cross, in the open side of the Redeemer,
and was manifested to the world on the day of Pentecost.*
At these two moments the Blessed Virgin was present as mother
of the Mystical Body of Jesus Christ. This Mystical Body

------

*Translator's Note. In this instance, also, Fray Colomer's words have been
recast in view of the content of the encyclical *Mystici Corporis,* paragraph 27,
which reads: "The Church which, already conceived, came forth from the side
of the second Adam in His sleep on the cross, first showed herself before
the eyes of men on the great day of Pentecost.... The Divine Redeemer ...
manifested and proclaimed [the Church] when He sent the Holy Ghost as
Paraclete in visible form on His disciples." The original text of Fray Colomer
in the passage above read: " ... the Mystical Body of Jesus Christ, or the supernatural society of souls ... was born on the day of Pentecost."

was conceived at the omnipotent word of Jesus; it was manifested in due time under the omnipotent action of the Holy Spirit. The Church, interiorly illumined and animated by the Holy Spirit and in her teachings assisted by Him, has always believed in her origin on Calvary, and has continually considered the mother of Jesus to be her own mother.

III

The relation of exemplar which we have previously considered in the Blessed Virgin with regard to the Church is wonderfully continued in Mary's maternity in respect to the Mystical Body of her Son. What wonder is it that the holy fruit of this spiritual maternity is seen in Jesus' mother, if this is the law of all generation in heaven and on earth? The spiritual maternity of the Blessed Virgin gives us another reason for the character of exemplar she possesses in relation to the Church. Yet the relationship of the Church to the Blessed Virgin does not end there.

In this world, the august functions of maternity gradually decrease until they are extinguished when the child reaches the fullness of its life and its lawful independence. The mother, who at first was everything for the child, gradually sees her maternal care limited with the organic and spiritual growth of the child. She it was who conceived her child and nourished him with her own blood until he was born. She it was who gave him the delicate food of her physical life with her milk, and the food of her spirit with Christian education. Yet the day arrives when lactation ceases, as also the food of the mother's soul ceases normally to animate the mature mind of the son or daughter. The formative action of the mother then converges into a love which follows her child always and which, as long as the mother lives, rests upon her offspring like the peaceful and generous kiss of roseate light with which the dawn breaks. This is the natural law as regards an earthly mother. That of the heavenly mother is just the opposite. The more the child grows the more he remains in the heart of his mother and the more he is nourished by what she gives him. This holds true for the Church and the Blessed Virgin with regard to each soul.

In effect: man is born into the Church through Baptism, yet he does not remain a being apart and distinct from the Church in the way a newly born child is with regard to his mother. Without losing his status as a person, the Christian remains vitally incorporated in Jesus within the Church. His every advancement in grace is a greater and deeper incorporation into the organic life of which he is a living member. The divine graces or influences which he receives, no matter how they have reached the soul, are aimed at placing it more deeply in the life of Jesus. The vital movement of the Christian is towards Jesus, the source of his human life and his life as a child of God, and not the opposite process, which is true in nature. The acme of the supernatural life is reached by the soul when it can truly repeat with the deep sentiment of the great Apostle: "It is now no longer I that live, but Christ lives in me."[8] In proportion to its union with Jesus, the soul is placed in, and deepened in, the life of the Church, and receives with greater vigor and effect the light of the Church's teaching authority, the direction of her governing body, the action of the Sacraments. These Christians fully submerged in and penetrated by the life of the Church are her most active parts. The life of the holy mother of the children of God is concentrated in them, with a most powerful force for radiation.

Something analogous takes place in the case of the Blessed Virgin. Through her mediation souls receive the divine life.

---
[8]Gal. 2:20.

The Blessed Virgin was associated with Jesus in the acquisition of this life through the redeeming sacrifice, and she is now an associate in the dispensing of the life gained on Calvary. Jesus, who associated His mother with Himself for the obtaining of the life of grace, did not have any reason to exclude her in its distribution. The maternity of the Blessed Virgin, therefore, had to be more than native, giving existence first to the Church in its apostolic generation, or better, to the whole Church at its origin on Calvary. Without functioning directly in regard to the generations which come into Christian life, the maternity of the Blessed Virgin had to entail also a mysterious repetition of the spiritual generation of each soul as it came to life as a child of God. This is required because of the universal association of the Blessed Virgin with the ministry of Jesus, which besides being a saving ministry is also a sanctifying one.

One may add to this the very delicate and ineffable relationship of the Blessed Virgin with the Holy Spirit. The Holy Spirit chose her for the human generation of Jesus, and she was, as Saint Louis Marie Grignon of Montfort says, repeating the words of Saint Augustine, a mold of Jesus under the action of the Holy Spirit. Thus the one who served as a pattern so that the Holy Spirit could form the Divine Head of the Mystical Body, would necessarily serve as a pattern for the formation of the mystical members of this Divine Head. The incomparable holiness of the Blessed Virgin, her inviolable fidelity to the Holy Spirit, whose spouse she is called by Christian piety, the prodigious power of her faculties — all these things make the Blessed Virgin a fit and holy subject whom the Holy Spirit might use as an admirable living channel for the dispensing of grace to souls. What is this dispensatory action of the Blessed Virgin as regards grace? We can fathom only a little of it. For who is capable of sounding out the mystery of this communication of life to souls through Jesus and Mary?

Undoubtedly the Blessed Virgin is our advocate and mediatrix in heaven. The sweet petitions of the Salve Regina put on the lips of the faithful what is the sentiment and unanimous voice of Tradition: We say to her every day, "Turn, then, most gracious advocate, thine eyes of mercy towards us." That is to say that in heaven the Blessed Virgin pleads for us, interceding with the heavenly Father by her prayer and merits, which are so intimately and inseparably united with those of Jesus and so fully in harmony with the plans of the Father, who "so loved the world that He gave His only-begotten Son."[9] The petitions of the Blessed Virgin in heaven are so mighty and the power of her merits so great and extensive that they gather into their sphere every soul and extend to them all grace. There is no reason that this grace should be limited. As there is no grace that does not come from the Holy Spirit, nor any that does not descend from Jesus, neither is there any grace that does not come to us through the mediation of the Blessed Virgin, associated with the Holy Spirit and with Jesus. Therefore, these gifts of God which bring to us the stream of divine life that it may become our supernatural life; these graces which shine like rays of light from heaven or shafts of sunlight from paradise sent that the divine flower might open and unfold its hidden splendor to the kisses of the eternal sun, come, by passing first — though we do not know exactly how — through the refined being of the Blessed Virgin, whose intellect, heart, and life pulsate in an ardent prayer that Divine Goodness may shower upon souls a copious supply of His mercies.

Theologians, admitting the truth of this mystery of universal intercession on the part of Mary, are not fully satisfied.

---

9 John 3:16.

The Christian heart sees more. Christian sentiment seems to glimpse, in the darkness of the mystery, something deeper, more profound, and, we might say, more vital, in this continual communication of grace through the Virgin Mary. Theological reason sharpens its powers to discover some new ray of light in the shadow of this mystery. It has recourse — in order to clarify the matter — to the mysterious yet very real action of the Sacraments; it scrutinizes the mystical experiences of souls who have themselves deeply experienced the delicate touch of the Blessed Virgin's action. We might say that here is a new world to discover and explore, that Christian sentiment, as it were, senses strange emanations of an action closer and deeper than the mediation that is assumed to be universal as regards souls and in graces; and that the warmhearted love of the Church for the sweet Mother of souls is extended to embrace more closely the Mother of heaven from whom the Church truly receives life. This is today a profound mystery which occupies the minds of theologians and attracts the hearts of the faithful. In time, perhaps, many hidden things will be clarified. In heaven we shall clearly see and know these things. We shall see in this mystery of the communication of divine life through the Blessed Virgin much more than we ever suspected; we shall profoundly experience, with a joy which cannot be expressed in words, the secret and vivifying touch of the Mother of God within us, as if it were the delicate hand of the Holy Spirit who puts life into whatever He touches.

However, if there is any obscurity on this point and any discord among theologians concerning the way in which the Blessed Virgin plays a part in the dispensation of graces to souls, there is none regarding the universality of her action. It is not a question of whether God can give His grace without the services of His mother. Divine power is not subject to any creature. But in the present order of Providence and in the

plan chosen by God for His work, Jesus and His mother are
at the center of the divine design and the source, as it were,
of all good for creatures, since in consideration of Jesus and
Mary all things were made and through divine bounty enriched. Hence Divine Goodness always makes use of Jesus'
sacred humanity and of the Blessed Virgin in the dispensing of
grace. This is enough for us. Christian hearts seem to expand
in breathing the fragrant air that comes to them from heaven
through the orchard of eternal flowers that is the Blessed
Virgin. Eyes seeking from above the light which secretly
"enlightens every man who comes into the world,"[10] are
refreshed and pleased at seeing it permeate the halo of gold
around the soul of the Blessed Virgin. Souls that yearn for
contact with the divine are filled with consolation as they
realize that the soft hand of this divine touch is the holy
Mother of Jesus and our Mother, too. What is known by
presentiment and conjecture in these delicate and hidden operations, the Church, without tearing away the veil of mystery
concerning the mode of the action of the Blessed Virgin in
souls, affirms, by her universal teaching authority, to be the
mediation of the Blessed Virgin in the distribution of graces.

Since, then, this truth is beyond doubt, let us draw from it
the very pleasing consequences it has for the Church.

The more that souls grow in grace, as we have previously
noted, the more they incorporate themselves into and penetrate
the life of the Church and the more intimately united with
Jesus they become. Necessarily, therefore, the more they come
under the action of the Blessed Virgin, the more fully and
profusely do they receive of the current of graces from her.
Growth in Christ is a development and increase in the stream
of life which comes to us from God through His mother.

---

10 John 1:9.

And since this is true for all souls, the whole Church, in the integrity of her social being, is constantly irrigated by this flourishing river of paradise, which perennially maintains the splendor of the spirit and the heavenly springtime of the divine life. One would look in vain for a member of the Church whom the holy influences of grace do not reach, or one whom they reach without passing through Mary. If one should try to find a moment in the existence of the Church in which the light of God fell upon her without being tinged with the very pure, crystal-like being of the Blessed Virgin, one would meet with failure. The Church finds herself, in her admirable unity and in the rich variety of her members, enveloped in and penetrated by the atmosphere which contains traces of the glory of the vivifying action of the Blessed Virgin.

Now the Blessed Virgin more than anyone else has participated in the life of Jesus and in the effusion of the Holy Spirit. The grace possessed by the Blessed Virgin is even more than that possessed by all the saints together. And we know that grace vitally unites one with Jesus in the unity of His Mystical Body. Hence the Blessed Virgin necessarily enters into, and is a principal part of, the great being which has Jesus for its Head and the Holy Spirit for its soul. What can she be or what can she represent in it?

Speaking of such profound realities, we must come back to comparisons and symbols taken from the world about us so that we can better say what we wish to express. Among these symbols of the Church, the most concise and expressive is that which has been called the anthropological one. The Church has frequently been compared by Saint Paul to a human organism and called the Mystical Body of Jesus Christ. In it the Blessed Virgin has an eminent place and function.

The living human organism possesses three essentials which act and influence universally: the soul, which animates the organism and causes it to live; the head, which regulates and directs every vital movement; and the heart, which incessantly beats as it sustains the organism by circulating throughout it vivifying blood. In the Mystical Body of Jesus the soul is the Holy Spirit; the Head, Jesus Christ; the heart, the Blessed Virgin. After the unity of the Holy Spirit and Jesus, is there a greater intimacy, a more continuous, universal, and necessary action than that of the heart of the Church?

Thus have been lightly sketched the most delicate and beautiful relationships which exist between the Church and the Blessed Virgin Mary.

CHAPTER III

THE CHURCH AND JESUS CHRIST

A S WE ascend in the hierarchy of beings in our considerations, the relationships of the Church with the sacred
and divine realities become more intimate and more compelling.
Notable and delicate are the bonds which she has with the
angels and the saints. Yet incomparably more eminent and
profound are those which she has with the Blessed Virgin, her
model, her mother, and her heart. Who, however, is able to
express in words the mysterious and ineffable relationship of
the Church with Jesus? We can do no more than stutter the
truths which the Lord has been pleased to reveal in order to
instruct us concerning this deep, mysterious, and intimate union
and compenetration between Jesus and the Church.

As best we can and with profound reverence, we shall
attempt to express these sacred relationships which exist between Jesus and His Church.

Jesus founded the Church. He chose the apostles, giving
them hierarchical powers which were to last forever, and
promising them His assistance until the consummation of the
world. The Church was born of Jesus, who died that He
might present to Himself a pure and immaculate Church, in
which there would be no wrinkle nor blemish.[1] The life of
the Church is centered on the unchangeable word of Jesus,
sustained by the secret action of her Founder, and protected

---

[1]Cf. Eph. 5:27.

117

by His omnipotent assistance against all enemies, both visible and invisible. All these things involve relationships which firmly bind the Church to Jesus, who is her origin and the permanent support of her life. Yet, because of our limited capacity to understand, they do not tell us all about the stupendous intimacy that exists between Jesus and the Church. We must have recourse to several symbols with which the Holy Spirit has enlightened us concerning this profound mystery of supernatural union. Among those symbols we choose three which can more vividly and efficaciously help us know what we are trying to understand. They are the terms Spouse or Bridegroom, Head, and Life of the Church as applied to Jesus. Jesus is the Divine Bridegroom of the Church, who is the Spouse of the Word made flesh; Jesus is Head of the Church, His Mystical Body; He is the Life of the Church, who knows and experiences this ineffable reality. Can more be said?

As a spouse the Church has a most exceptional relationship with Jesus, expressed in the relationship of Eve to Adam. Eve came to life formed by God from the substance of Adam. Hence in unfolding itself, the mighty potential power of the first man, under the divine action, became capable of increasing the number of members in the human family. The Church was born of Jesus, when, after the side of the Divine Bridegroom had been opened on the cross, there trickled forth the last drops of blood and water He possessed — a mysterious symbol of the sacraments which give divine life to the children of Adam in order to change them into children of God. The Divine Spouse was born in this way from the heart of her Bridegroom, that she might be His helpmate in all things and the mother of His children.

Since the Church was formed to be the Spouse of Jesus Christ, she had to receive from her Divine Bridegroom the dignity and status which would bring her to the level of spouse, and the rights which such a dignity and union entail. Jesus is the Son of the eternal Father. The Church must be the daughter of God. Jesus is God and is filled with divine life in His sacred humanity. The Church must be elevated to the divine order and filled with the Holy Spirit, who is the Spirit of her Bridegroom. Because of His dignity and merits, Jesus is King of creation and Lord of all that exists. The Church must be a Queen to her Bridegroom and Mistress of all that falls under His jurisdiction. Saint Paul speaks to us of the sovereign action of God subjecting all things to the limitless authority of God's Son made man.[2] Good order demands that the Church should take part in the universal sovereignty of her Bridegroom. Jesus did not choose the Church as a slave, but as a loving Spouse for whom He has given His blood.[3] Would He deny her the dignity and rights of a queen which are hers because of her indissoluble and holy union with Jesus?

No human society has or can have a similar relationship with Jesus. God has subjected everything to the sovereignty of His Son made man. Hence Jesus is King of the nations and Lord of those who govern and rule them. Only the Church, among the societies on earth, ascends the throne with Jesus and thus possesses a dignity above all human dignity. The day will come in which the dependence of all creation on the Church will be manifest to all. This will have to be recognized and accepted by all either through love or through the power of Jesus Christ's dominion. Yet this dominion is no less real now, although human pride or daring ignorance may seek to deny it. Because of her dignity, the Church is above all the powers in the world; these, for the purpose of being properly

---

[2] Cf. I Cor. 15:26; Heb. 2:8.   [3] Cf. Eph. 5:25.

ordered, must be subject as regards the source of their power and its exercise, to the eminent law of moral life which the holy Spouse of Jesus Christ teaches with infallible authority.

This is the order of things, based on the dignity and the status of the Church. But if blinded minds and proud hearts rebelled against Jesus Himself and, throwing off His holy and sweet yoke, crucified the Redeemer, is it strange that inflamed ignorance and pride should rise in fury against the Church and desire to exile her from the world and to efface her holy footprints? Jesus has given His Spouse the mysterious gift of His sorrows and His cross. A thousand times He has reminded His generous followers that after His grace He has no better gift for the soul than the cross. What is true with regard to the individual members of the Church is incomparably more true regarding the Mystical Body as a whole. Through the mysterious design of Love, supernatural fruitfulness is associated with the bloody sacrifice of Jesus. The latter involved the painful birth of the children of God. Jesus has given the same fruitfulness to His Church, which was associated with Him in His tremendous sacrifice. Through the sacrifice of the cross Jesus communicates the first ray of divine life to all who are born of Him for God. Through the continual sacrifice of the Church, the holy Spouse of Jesus Christ plants the field of the world with the flowers of life and populates heaven with holy souls. If, by being the Spouse of Jesus, the Church has received the dignity and life of a Spouse with the precious gift of her Bridegroom's love, she has also received from Him the treasure of the cross, which the hatred of the world and of the demons of hell obstinately and indefatigably prepare for her.

Such similarity between faithful Spouse and Bridegroom could not fail to exist. The Church now seems to be like Jesus in His sufferings, because she is called to enter into the glory of her Bridegroom on the same road of pain which Jesus had to follow in order to enter into His glory.[4] In dignity, in holiness, in pain, in the fruitfulness of her sacrifice and in the rights which follow from them, the Church is the living copy of Jesus; she is His divine Spouse, born from His open side on the cross, and His faithful helper in all things.

Jesus and the Church are spouses indissolubly united in life and inseparably associated in dignity and action.

II

The images and comparisons we have used in order to explain what Jesus is to the Church do not tell all that is involved in the relations between these two. Hence we must use other images and comparisons in order that one may be completed by another, and that we may derive from these a better knowledge of the vital compenetration between Jesus and the Church.

We have explained what is included in the relationship or symbol of Spouse when applied to the Church with regard to Jesus. The Church is a helpmate formed by God for His Son, with whom she is united by an inextinguishable love and the same interests and ministry. Yet a spouse, no matter how intimate and closely united to her bridegroom in thought, sentiment, and work is something distinct from him and not a part of his life as an individual. The Church is more than this with regard to Jesus. The union of the two reaches the mystical unity of being. Jesus is the living Head of His Church and the Church is His Mystical Body. This is undoubtedly much more than is signified by matrimony. In matrimony there is a communication of the name and dignity of the bridegroom to his wife, a common life, common interests and affections, and moral unity in the diminutive society of the family. Yet the

---

4Cf. Luke 24:26.

matrimonial union does not extend to unity of physiological life
between the spouses, as if they were one, living, and complete
being. Between Jesus and the Church there is indeed, mystically, this living unity which is not duplicated anywhere; nor
is there similarity in any other case. Jesus is the Head; the
Church, the body of this Divine Head. A single supernatural
life animates and joins the two. Jesus is God and from Him,
as the Father, proceeds the Holy Spirit, who fills and supernaturally vivifies the sacred humanity of Jesus. From the Son
this life is diffused and spread through the Church, animating
her and giving her the divine being she possesses in its
admirable unity, rich variety, and solid organization, and
causing her to live according to Jesus and for Jesus, and as if
Jesus were her own intimate life. The life of the Church is
the same supernatural life as that of the sacred humanity, now
mysteriously transferred to the Church's members. The ideas
and infallible evaluations of Jesus are what, through revealed
doctrine and the continual assistance of the Holy Spirit, en-
lighten, illustrate, and nourish the Church with truth. The
sentiments of the Redeemer, the affections and desires of His
heart are poured into the Church and thus beat and exist in
her heart. The Church has no other sentiments. All her
divine strength comes from Jesus; that is, all the graces which
sustain her in her life, those which move her to the conquest
of souls, defend her against her enemies, and sustain her firmly
in her desire and work. And in spite of the great weight of
human weaknesses in her members which she bears, these
graces flow from Jesus as an inextinguishable current of life
coming from an inexhaustible source.

In the human organism, the head is the eminent organ of
life in which resides fullness of thought and the sensory and
motor centers of the whole body. The head operates in harmony with the sense organs, though the latter are distant from

it in the organism. The voluntary and the many involuntary and unconscious movements of the other members begin in the head. It is the principal and dominant organ to which others are subjected and of which they are tributaries. Even the orderly and proportionate growth of the members of the body has its roots in the nerve centers of the head, the directors of the regulated development of tissues, organs, and limbs. The head is a very important and necessary organ in the human body. The whole body depends upon it. Everything is an extension of the action of the head.

This tells us much more about the influx of Jesus in the Church than does the symbol of matrimony, the idea of two spouses as applied to Jesus and His Church. In what moment of life does the head cease to influence the organism it dominates and directs? At what point can one cut off, without destroying the body, this varied communication and direction of the head in the body? Whether we are awake or asleep, this action in the human organism never ceases. Whether we who live in the Church know it or not, the holy influx of Jesus in His Mystical Body is never interrupted, in order that He may gradually form this Body according to His being and regulate all its supernatural activities and operations, no matter how small and hidden they may be. No matter how fleeting or how permanent a sensation of ours may be, the organ capable of perceiving it and the cerebral center partake in it. In like manner, there is no living and divine work in the Church, no matter who has performed it, in which Jesus does not partake, as Head. The tears of repentance shed by an unknown sinner, the secret desire of a soul that wishes to give itself to Jesus, the sigh of love from another, like a fiery dart piercing the heart of God, the hidden endeavor of immolation on the part of a soul wishing to master itself for God, the piercing word of an apostle knocking on the doors of a heart that it might be opened to the action of divine grace, the sacramental action exercised in Baptism, in the pardoning of a sinner who confesses, in Holy Communion — all that is supernaturally performed in the Church is the work of her Divine Head, Jesus Christ. It is He who performs in and through His members each and every one of the actions of life found in His Mystical Body.

It would be a pleasing thing for a soul who loves Jesus to experience the holy glance of her Lover following her everywhere. Everything the soul does, she would see in the light of Jesus' loving glance. But what really happens is more than this, although we do not experience it or see it. The glance of Jesus certainly follows us everywhere, and His divine action penetrates everything supernatural that we do. Our good works are His and our own, His even more than ours because of the full knowledge with which He performs them and because of the sovereignty of His authority over them. Whenever the action of Jesus does not extend to our own acts, there is no life in them. They are dead, hidden corners into which our weakness or malice has not allowed the light of Jesus to enter. Whatever our acts have of what is supernaturally good, beneficial, and vital comes from Jesus and in Jesus has the root of its power and vigor. The action of the Divine Head of the Church thus penetrates our Christian life and the life of the whole Mystical Body. If the action of Jesus in the Church were an aroma, the whole being of the Church and all her acts would give forth the penetrating and pleasing fragrance of Jesus. If it were a beautiful melody, all the acts of the Church would harmonize in Jesus. If it were a light, all the works of the Church and the supernatural works of her members would glow with rays coming from Jesus.

Among these actions are the ministerial ones; that is, those of the Church as a living body made up of members ordained for a sacred ministry. Furthermore, there are the charismatic actions; namely, those of an individual member who fulfills his Christian duties or performs his acts in a Christian manner, even to the most humble and those seemingly most remote and most separated from the divine life. In all these actions Jesus operates and exerts influence. If Peter baptizes, said Saint Augustine, Jesus baptizes. We might say: "If Peter pardons, it is Jesus who pardons in Peter; if Peter consecrates, preaches or blesses, it is Jesus who consecrates, preaches, and blesses." If this vital communication with Jesus is severed, the fruitful sacramental rites would be useless formulas and sterile ceremonies. If Jesus should withdraw His vivifying action from the ministerial function of the Church, it would be sterile, without power or efficacy to sanctify a soul, to move a heart towards God. Thanks to the constant and secret action of Jesus, the ministry of the Church is inexhaustibly fruitful, her action is a source of divine life and her atmosphere a healthy and a propitious one for souls.

Just as the ministries of the Church are fruitful through Jesus, so are the supernatural works of the members of the Church. In the ministerial actions, the influence of Jesus is never lacking, though the minister may be a poor sinner. In the ordinary works of the Christian, the action of Jesus does not extend to the work performed by the member if the latter has by sin destroyed his vital union with Jesus, or if his work, because it is sinful, repeals the supernatural vivification. Yet if the Christian does not put actual or habitual sin in the way, his good works bear the stamp of Jesus, the fragrance of His life, the strength of His spirit, and the power of the impulse of the Divine Head. No matter how humble and small such acts are, they bear the mark of Jesus, which gives them divine value and supernatural force; and, once brought onto the field of life, these actions are not like unproductive grain thrown into a furrow or a senseless shout in the desert. They are a living power in the world of souls and in the divine harmony of creation, a note attuned to the other divine melodies in the invisible world of souls. They are, in a word, the acts of a Christian whose roots of life are in Jesus and whose supernatural power comes from Him.

Thus does Jesus penetrate the whole being of the Church through His Spirit, and thus does His action permeate all the supernatural works of the Church, ministerial or charismatic, public or private, performed by the Church as a society or by an unknown member in the Church's organism.

Such a compenetration between Jesus and the Church brings it about that what belongs to Jesus is attributed to and spoken of as belonging to the Church, and what belongs to the Church as belonging to Jesus. Jesus acts and suffers in His members: He performs their Christian works and suffers their pains, persecutions, and losses. He it is who sanctifies everything in His Church: her actions, her desires, her sufferings.

It is said that a nun, doubting the virtue of Saint Catherine of Ricci, uncharitably disturbed and annoyed her. One day she saw the face of the saint transfigured, so that it had the appearance of the face with which the Saviour is usually represented. She saw that the eyes of this strange countenance looked at her compassionately and seriously, and she heard from the lips these words: "Why do you mistreat me?" It was the dramatic reproduction of Jesus' words to Paul on the way to Damascus: "Why dost thou persecute Me? . . . I am Jesus whom thou art persecuting."[5] Jesus, truly living in the Church whose Head He is, does what is divinely performed in the Church, and suffers whatever in His name and in union with Him the Church and her members suffer.

---

[5] Acts 9:4-5.

III

We have not as yet exhausted our subject, nor have we arrived at the depths of the mystery. Jesus is more than head: He is the life of the Church. Yet the more deeply we penetrate our subject, the more arduous and difficult its exposition becomes, insofar as our poor human minds, illumined by grace, can comprehend it. Saint Paul, profoundly moved, speaking of his intimate union with Jesus, said: "It is now no longer I that live, but Christ lives in me";[6] "For me to live is Christ."[7] With profound meaning he said to the Colossians: "For you have died and your life is hidden with Christ in God. When Christ, your life, shall appear, then you too will appear with Him in glory."[8] There is between Jesus and His living members — and, with greater reason, between Jesus and His Church — such a bond and such compenetration of lives that one cannot explain it in the light of the matrimonial relationship or express it completely by saying Jesus is our head and we are His members. It is necessary to say that He is our life; that, in our language, He is deeply incorporated in our existence. Is there perhaps anything more intimately and truly our own than our life? It is the root, the subject, and the center of everything we have. When a man loses it, everything in this world is lost to him. When life is gone, the value and meaning of other things disappear, since only life, with its needs and ends, gives them the value they have for us.

Yet there is more. The supernatural life in the depths of our spirit destined to dominate and rule us is certainly the most profound thing that can be given to us, an intangible good which cannot be snatched away by the adverse powers that can take away other goods from us. Through an un-

---

[6]Gal. 2:20.   [8]Col. 3:3-4.
[7]Phil. 1:21.

fortunate event or compelled by necessity, we can lose a member of our body without losing our life. Old age, infirmity, a disastrous accident can take away life, and no one has the power to avoid such an evil. Everything in the world can be lost through some act of violence or through some inevitable natural catastrophe. But this does not hold true for the supernatural life. Neither Satan with his power and fury, nor the world with its poisonous malice, nor human tyranny which can take away our liberty, trample on our rights, or snatch away our life in the midst of torments, is capable of plunging a hand into the depths of the spirit where the divine life is established and violently extirpating it, as men have violently carved up the bodies of the martyrs. In this sense we say that the supernatural life is the most profound thing we have and the greatest and most profound good in our being. When we leave this earthly life, the heavenly life becomes rooted in the soul with greater vigor, so that it is inviolable and imperishable under all circumstances. Nothing nor anyone can deprive us of this divine good. Only sin can destroy this treasure; only sin contains enough corrosive power to kill the divine life placed in the soul by Baptism.

Now this life, so deep, so interior and so inviolable in the face of extraneous forces, is Jesus made our own life. This life becomes established in the spiritual roots of our being and puts into our will such a delicate bond of love between the soul and God that no one except the sanctified man himself, with his free will, is capable of uprooting this divine plant from the soul. Not even the devil with his keenness of intellect can fathom this hidden mystery of the divine life. It is God living in us and making us partakers of His essentially divine nature.[9] It is God coming into our soul through Jesus Christ and infusing Himself into us as a new life to make us

---

9Cf. II Peter 1:4.

live according to Jesus. It is the Spirit of Jesus incorporating Himself into our being and causing to flow there, from Jesus to us, the thoughts and affections of the Saviour. He thus sets up between Jesus and us such an intimate and vital bond that when it is experienced the soul must utter those surprising words of Saint Paul: "It is now no longer I that live, but Christ lives in me."[10] Who can say what this is like? What faith tells us obscurely, the saints experience in raptures of intimate union with Jesus. We too shall experience it pleasingly and gloriously in heaven. Until we are there, however, we shall not be able to explain clearly this stupendous penetration in which Jesus becomes our life, to the point where love sees all its dreams fulfilled, chimerical in the human order, but become a reality in the divine.

And since life penetrates and animates the whole living being, when Jesus is truly the life of the soul and the soul allows itself to be completely penetrated by Him, the whole human being is incorporated in Jesus. Thus everything in the human being has a most extraordinary value, as befits one who is touched by and made holy in and through Jesus.

This is true of a soul in grace, especially of the soul that knows how, and seeks, to live for Jesus. Yet it is incomparably more true of the great being of the Church, which will never be without the life of Jesus. The Church can always and truthfully say: "It is now no longer I that live but Christ lives in me";[11] because she knows no other life. Jesus exists in her thoughts and in her teachings, and the Church never departs from Him. Jesus lives in the affections of the Church. Hence there is no sentiment in the Church which is not united with those of the heart of Jesus. Jesus is the norm of the Church's social conscience and the internal law which governs

---

[10]Gal. 2:20.   [11]Ibid.

her life. Jesus is everything to the Church. He is her substance and her life, so that her whole being is neither more nor less than Jesus extended in His mystical members: "the completion of Him who fills all with all."[12] Men have found no word that can better express this profound truth and delicate compenetration than the word *life*. For this reason the Church says with the great Apostle: "Christ lives in me." The Church need only submerge herself in her own living reality to find Jesus. She need only act, to exercise her divine powers of radiating Jesus; she need only speak — that is, say what comes from her heart to her lips — to preach Jesus. He fills her mind, her heart, her entire life. Jesus is her treasure. In Jesus she has all, and outside Him she neither seeks nor wants anything. If Jesus left the Church, she would die. With Jesus she is invincible and immortal, though everything else perishes and the world crumbles at her feet. She has a prayer that never ceases; but this prayer passes through the heart of her Bridegroom. She is unable to pray except in and through Jesus. She has a sacrifice which she offers every day in every part of the world, but this sacrifice is Jesus Himself. Could it be otherwise? When Jesus desired to make the universal religious offering of His great ministry, He made of His own being a victim, and of His own life a sacrifice consummated on the cross. When, diffused in His Church, He wished to give her a sacrifice, He gave Himself as a Eucharistic Victim, and He gave to His Church the power of immolating the Victim bloodlessly. In order that the Church might live according to Jesus, and that Jesus might be the nucleus, the form, and the substance of her life, the sacrifice had to be Jesus Himself, in conformity with the status of the one who would offer the sacrifice — the Church.

12Eph. 1:23.

Since the Church is so constituted, Jesus being her light of truth, the object of her love, and her life, could the Church nourish herself with other bread or food than Jesus Christ? The Christian mind moves towards, and the the heart touched by grace tends towards, this good of the life of the sanctified man, that is, the Eucharist. How could the life that lives in Jesus be nourished, if not with Jesus? The Divine Founder and Master of the Church was able to provide for the desire which throughout time would appear in the Church. And with an unheard-of delicacy He left her a food capable of satisfying the insatiable hunger of love which desires to be nurtured on the loved one and to grow in His life.

Since Jesus is the profound and immortal life of the Church, could she cease to live totally for Him? No, she could not. This is her desire, this is her law, and this is the principle which sums up her whole history.

IV

Let us briefly consider this last point. Jesus said that a man could have no greater and more generous love than that of giving up his life for a friend.[13] And Saint Paul, speaking of the love of Jesus for His Church, says that "Christ also loved the Church and delivered Himself up for her."[14] Jesus carried His love for the Church to that eminent point of perfection where He gave her a burning and consuming love. In forming her Himself, He showed that He loved the Church with a generous and inextinguishable ardor. And when once she was formed, He kept on following her and loving her in this same way. Who can say what love Jesus has for His Church? Speaking to Saint Catherine of Genoa concerning the

---

[13]Cf. John 15:13.   [14]Eph. 5:25.

great love of His divine heart for the saint, Jesus said: "If
you could but know how much I love you, it would be the
last thing you would know, for such a joy would kill you."
Saint Catherine was but a tiny part in the immense living
organism of the Church. We might list the thousands and
millions of souls in the Church to whom Jesus could repeat
the pleasing words He spoke to the saint. We might amass all
these very wonderful acts of assistance and regard with which
love has inspired Jesus in regard to hundreds and thousands of
souls: the exchange of hearts; the marks of His wounds; the
mysterious reproduction of the pains of His Passion; change
of interests. We might exert the mind to draw out the delicate
substance of all the burning phrases of Jesus to those who love
Him and His greatest familiarities with them. Yet if we could
do all these things, we would scarcely have said anything
about this love of God and of God made man burning in the
Divine Heart of Jesus.

When in the many brilliant letters of light, in the form
of the blessed and the angels of heaven, we shall read, in the
day of eternity, the stupendous poem of the Church, manifested before our amazed eyes in the splendor of glory, we
shall know, without understanding it, the love of Jesus for
His Church. All the marvels of heaven caused by God are a
display of His love. Yet this love is greater than all these
things together, because their inherent limitation is, as it
were, a vase too small for the rich essence of Jesus' love.
It would be necessary to gather from the lives of the saints
all the burning words with which the love of Jesus for souls
has inspired them, in order to stammer even the least that
could be said about it with words. Concerning this love of
Jesus for His Church, it is appropriate to paraphrase here the
statement of St. Paul: "Eye has not seen, nor ear heard, nor
has it entered into the heart of man what is the love of Jesus

for His Church."[15] Stars vanish from the sky at break of day. Once the sun has appeared on the horizon and once it begins to rise high in the heavens, the stars cannot be seen, since they are hidden from our eyes by the triumphant light of the sun. The ardent love of the saints, the abounding power of their love for Jesus — which has sometimes reached the strange degree of expanding the breast and breaking the ribs, as in the case of Saint Philip Neri; of piercing hearts, changing love into a mysterious dart, like the one with which the Seraphim transfixed the heart of Saint Theresa; of impressing Jesus' wounds on the members of the body, as in the case of Saint Francis of Assisi — is like the light of these stars in the blue sky, pleasing and constant, yet effaced by the dazzling light of the sun: the love of Jesus for His Church. Is it strange, then, that one who loved the Church thus would deliver Himself up to the death on the cross that she might live? Can we be amazed when we realize that Jesus gave the Church His Spirit for her soul, the Eucharist as a sacrifice and a food, and His heart for a treasure? In Jesus, love reached that peak which it is not given to our poor minds to understand. It moved Him to do things which astound the saints and which will amaze us when — once the earthly scales which blind our eyes have disappeared — we shall see, in the light of glory, what it is given us to comprehend in this immense abyss of life and glory in the Heart of Jesus Christ. Such is the love Jesus has for His Church.

How does the Church love Jesus? She cannot love Him in the same degree that He loves her, for she has not this capacity to love. But insofar as she can, the Church loves Jesus wholeheartedly. Certainly, there are some members of the Church who do not love our Lord or who only superficially

---

15Cf. I Cor. 2:9.

and egotistically direct their hearts to Him. However, these cold or dead members do not constitute the Church as a social and holy body: they are her weak and infirm part, and not the organism of inexhaustible and vibrant life. Since the latter organism is animated by the Holy Spirit, directed by Jesus as its Head, necessarily holy in its doctrine, sacraments, and government, it has to be such in the indestructible unity of its being; and it bears within itself thousands of souls who heroically love Jesus, souls in whom the power of the spirit seems to be concentrated. Such is the love that the Church has for her Bridegroom. If all Christian souls would generously dispose themselves for the vivifying action of the Church, they would fervently love Jesus with marvelous force and heroic abnegation. The life of the Church has this power: it has, of itself, the capacity to awaken extraordinary energies and to enkindle the divine and consuming fire of charity in souls. Since there will never be lacking in the Mystical Body of Jesus Christ souls who give themselves over to this love, it is through them that we trace the love of the Church for Jesus; for the life of the Church and the impelling power of her love shine and are plainly shown in them. Such souls are unable to deny Jesus anything. They are the fitting fuel of the consuming flame of love of God. Their desire is to deny themselves for love of Him who humbled Himself for us; their wish is to serve and love wholeheartedly Him who first loved us even to dying on the cross and giving us the Eucharist. Saint Francis de Sales said that if he knew that in his heart there were a fiber which did not love Jesus, he would unhesitatingly tear it out. The feeling of this lovable saint is shared by all the saints. They have lived for Jesus and their desire has been to consecrate their life to Him and to make their actions acknowledge Him. If it has been necessary to deny themselves heroically, they have done so; if it has been necessary to perform harsh penances, they have not shrunk from the way of immolation. If the love of Jesus has demanded painful sacrifices, they have ardently embraced what destroys the desires and passions of nature. Their joy has been to live for Jesus, to allow His life to pervade and to penetrate them profoundly and entirely and to have Him as the hidden mainspring of their will in its acts of love.

When this habitual, self-denying, and generous love is enlivened and grows, when under the holy pressure of Jesus the soul gains new strength and its ardor is enkindled, it is capable of heroic works which astound, and spiritual abandonment which the purest human love cannot attain. Then zeal for the interests of Jesus is not lacking in the hearts of these Christians who are habitually heroic. Their efforts are limited to giving free reign to their ardent love. Penances are accepted as spiritual gifts and as an alleviation. They desire martyrdom as if it were a refreshing bath in the flames which burn and consume. They experience holy words of encouragement and cries of love which move the most profound depths of their being. They seem to be hearts into which Jesus has poured the burning desires of His own heart and which, not being able to hold them, break forth into cries of supernatural affection and inconceivable love. Thus Saint Francis of Assisi wept and caused others to do so because Love is not loved; Saint Dominic Guzman thirsted for martyrdom and Saint Anthony of Padua sailed to Africa in search of it. Thus Saint Theresa with captivated countenance was interiorly overcome with love and pain as a result of being pierced by the golden dart with a flaming point. Who could count the number of flaming hearts that exist and have existed in the Church? Who will be able to paint vividly and colorfully this stupendous force of love which sends souls to heaven with such incredible power or carries them throughout the world like firebrands to enkindle other souls? If we reduce to unity of being and of life all hearts made burning and living love, their number increases with the millions of sincere Christians who place the will and desire of God above all things and who live entirely submissive to this standard. If we make of it all one being from whom comes forth this life that sends out living sparks and that is capable of arousing them in all those who generously and selflessly receive such life, in this inviolable unity of life and of love and in these ineffable desires manifested in thousands of ways by abnegation and sacrifice — all this is what we now comprehend about the love of the Church for Jesus.

The Church lives in and for Jesus. A fervent Christian may sometimes fail; the Church will never fail in her burning love for Jesus. A good Christian may fall and be unfaithful; the Church cannot be separated from the heart of her Bridegroom, nor can she lag in her devotion. The centuries roll by, institutions grow old, the circumstances of human life change. What does not pass, or grow old, or change is the powerful and fervent affection of the Church for Jesus. Loving her Bridegroom as she does, who can do anything against her? Earthly powers may take away her possessions, they may deny her rights, they may tyrannize over her; what no one can do is to destroy her heart or take away from her the love for her Spouse. The more she is molested and persecuted, the more her generous love is manifested, and the more magnificent, pure, and ardent are the flames of her charity. There is no power that can go against that power. Speaking to His apostles at the Last Supper, Jesus said: "In the world you will have affliction. But take courage, I have overcome the world."[16] The Church, loving Jesus constantly and untiringly, can repeat,

---

16John 16:33.

addressing her children, the triumphant words of her Bridegroom: "Fear not; my love overcomes all the powers of the world and of hell." From this love have come forth all her heroic works, which run into the millions; from it will constantly bud forth, until the consummation of the world, generous acts which amaze mankind and examples of sacrifice whose root and power cannot be of this world. If Jesus has loved the Church to the extent of the cross and the Eucharist, the Church loves Jesus to the point of martyrdom.

This burning and close bond of love is the consummation of the profound, vital, and mysterious relations between Jesus and His Church. Such deep, penetrating, and holy relations could not have any other seal than this burning love of Jesus for His Church and of His Church for Him.

CHAPTER IV

THE CHURCH AND THE BLESSED TRINITY

IN THIS chapter we arrive at the sacred fountains of supernatural life and the magnificent heights where the Church
is submerged in the splendors of divine life. At each step of our
ascent on the ladder of beings, we have discovered marvelous
relationships and unsuspected beauty in the Church. Just as a
small cloud suspended on the horizon in the radiant hour of
dawn is submerged in light — penetrated, enveloped, and
illumined by the first rays of the sun — so too the Church,
once we have arrived at this point of our study, seems to be
placed in the immense sea of divine light and thus remain
full and resplendent in the immortal clarity which eternally
circulates, without movement or succession, from the Father
to the Son and from the Son to the Holy Spirit.

With reverent fear, like that of Moses in the dazzling
cloud of Sinai, we shall enter this mysterious cloud of light
and fire and there contemplate Holy Mother Church as placed
within the sacred splendors of the most holy Trinity.

I

The first relationship we must consider in this chapter is
that which the Church has with the Holy Spirit.

The Holy Spirit is subsistent Love and personal Holiness,
the author of all holiness and the penetrating and profound
source of every supernatural work. The Church is the work-
manship of the Holy Spirit. From Him she receives life and

138

power of action; in Him she subsists with indestructible stability and immortal life.

The Holy Spirit proceeds from the Father and the Son in the inviolable unity of the divine essence. He is sent by the Son to complete and bring to its consummation the supernatural elevation of creation and the divine rehabilitation of mankind. This outstanding grace was merited by the bloody sacrifice of Jesus, which was totally directed, in what concerns us, to the communication of the Holy Spirit to souls in the unity of the Church. In virtue of this communication, the Church both exists and is what she is.

The Holy Spirit fills the Church completely. There is no true member of the Church whom He has not stamped with His sacred seal. When the Holy Spirit is infused into a soul for the first time through Baptism, He not only vivifies it, but also stamps it with an indelible spiritual character. The character which He imprints upon the soul and which the soul will never lose is the baptismal character. Even in adults who receive Baptism validly, though not its grace because of being badly disposed, this character is firmly engraved and enchased as a proper effect of Baptism. Thus its subject is marked forever as a sacred possession of God, supernaturally dedicated to Him, and sealed by the priesthood of Jesus Christ, which qualifies it, as a member of the Mystical Body of the Redeemer, for reception of the sacraments and the integral life of the Church.

For this reason the influence of the Holy Spirit is universal in the Church; and there is no member whom He does not reach, though many of them are living in sin.

Yet the action of the Holy Spirit in the Church is not, and cannot be, limited to this divine mark which signifies and designates secretly the children of God and makes them members of the Church. The work of the Spirit is a work of life.

When he imprints this character upon all the baptized, He also pours forth the supernatural life in the well-disposed who do not place any obstacle to its reception. He vivifies them divinely with the life of God, making them children of adoption, partakers of the divine nature, with a right to the glorious inheritance of the heavenly Father and with family ties with the Divine Persons and with all others vivified by God. There is no member in the Church who does not receive life from the sacred fountain of the Holy Spirit. There is not a trace of life in the Mystical Body of Jesus which does not proceed from the animating Spirit whom Jesus sends to His Spouse in order that He may be the soul that animates her and sustains her in life.

The action of the Holy Spirit in the Church does not come about by chance, but rather is the means of wisely dispensing the divine gifts, which qualify each member for a personal function that is well co-ordinated and united with the functions of the rest, in the organic unity of the Church. Depending on this gift, each Christian receives his share of divine life in the Mystical Body of Jesus Christ and the charisms or graces of general use necessary that each personal gift might fit harmoniously into the organism whose member he is. Order and hierarchy in the members of the Church and the co-ordination of activities in the Church, directed towards the formation of saints, are not marvels, therefore, but rather a necessary result of this wise dispensation of gifts and charisms.

Since the Church is thus vitally constituted by the vivifying presence of the Holy Spirit, the Church is not left to her own human powers and efforts. Rather, she is assisted and sustained in everything, in her being, in her life, and in her work, by the omnipotent Spirit of Jesus. Just as the soul that animates us assists and manifests itself even in the smallest operations of our organic life, so does the Holy Spirit assist and operate in the Church in all that she does and in all that is done in her. There is no holy act performed by her most hidden and humble member in which the action of the Holy Spirit is not present. He is present in the silent prayer that rises to heaven, in the selfless abnegation of a soul that gives itself to God, in the word of eternal life which comes forth from a Christian heart, in the repentance which turns a prodigal son towards his home, in the blessing which a priest imparts to persons, to things animated and inanimated, in the preaching of the word of God, in mysterious and life-giving sacramental operations. The Church has no living work or ministerial function in which the Holy Spirit does not apply His sanctifying power and in which He does not leave the trace of life in souls. All the Church's life is sustained by the Holy Spirit and all her rich activity is animated, directed, and made fruitful through Him who is the soul of the Mystical Body. The Church teaches, sanctifies, and governs. But at the root of all these ministries can be found the vivifying action of the Holy Spirit. The Church prays, blesses, consecrates, and offers to God the Eucharistic sacrifice. But the Spirit of Jesus, who gives these operations the powerful efficacy they possess, acts in the depths of these sacred functions. He inspired, at the proper time, the truths of eternal life which He thought it well to entrust to the ecclesiastical teaching authority as the treasure of the Church. He assists the Pope and the episcopal body that they may not err when teaching and that, in the development of doctrine in which contact with the human intelligence is involved, no earthly elements may creep in to contaminate the pure stream of the divine waters.

The Holy Spirit sustains the Church. And the Church lives and subsists in Him immortally and unfailingly. It is the Holy Spirit who, putting the impress of Jesus on each soul and making it live in and through Jesus, causes the whole Church to be a splendid extension of the life of Jesus Christ and of His admirable Mystical Body. If the Holy Spirit withdrew from the Church, she would be powerless and dead. What would remain of society would be doomed to be reduced to dust and to dissolve through the weakness of human things, as would a body which has lost the unifying bond of life and the internal power of action and development. If the Church lives, prospers, spreads, and sends forth rays of life, and resists unfailingly the wild assaults of her enemies and the dissolvent poison of corruption from her own members, it is the work of the immortal Spirit who animates her and who is the sacred fulfillment of Jesus' promise to be with her until the consummation of the world.

The Archangel Gabriel, in his message to the Virgin concerning the Incarnation, said: "The Holy Spirit shall come upon thee and the power of the Most High shall overshadow thee."[1] With due allowance we can truly apply these words to the Church. The Holy Spirit overshadowed her on the great day of Pentecost, and He has not deserted her from that moment. The power from on high has been incorporated in her and thus gives her the perennial fruitfulness with which she indefatigably conceives, brings to light, and rears innumerable children of God. The whole Church is mysteriously penetrated by the Holy Spirit who vivifies her and who causes to come forth, from all her living parts — wherever they may be, in heaven, on earth, and in purgatory — this rich current of life in the continual beneficent circulation which is called the communion of saints. Everything that lives and acts supernaturally in the Church does so through the Holy Spirit. Everything that vitally belongs to the Church she possesses through the living bond of the Spirit. Everyone divinely marked as

---

[1]Luke 1:35.

belonging to the Church and living her life has been thus marked by the Holy Spirit. Jesus, the Blessed Virgin, the angels and the saints, the souls in purgatory, the members of the Church in this world are everything that they are in the supernatural order, through the action of the Holy Spirit. Through this action the Church finds herself more or less enveloped or submerged in a sea of light, in the life which comes forth from the mysterious depths of personal Love and eternally subsistent Holiness.

II

The Church, born of the sacrifice of Jesus, animated by the Holy Spirit, and directed by Jesus as Head, must necessarily move surely and firmly towards the heavenly Father, the eternal Source of life in heaven and on earth. The eternal Father engenders the Son, to whom He communicates everything save His personal quality as Father, which is essentially incommunicable. The Son receives everything from the Father: substance, intelligence, love, and power of action. And since these are of the Father, the Father lives and remains immanently in the Son and the Son in the infinitely fruitful heart of the Father. From both the Father and the Son proceeds the Holy Spirit; He is the personal Holiness of both and the power of infinite Love which unites them in an infinitely glorious embrace in the unity of nature of the three Divine Persons. The great, eternal, and glorious circulation of life thus goes from the Father to the Son and from them to the Holy Spirit, without ever becoming exhausted. In the heart of the Blessed Trinity life is the light of truth, the flame of love, and ineffable spiritual joy in constant and glorious circulation.

From this unapproachable height the supernatural life descends to souls within the Church. As Jesus has said: "God so loved the world that He gave His only-begotten Son."[2] This merciful effusion of the love of the Father is the Church; that is, Jesus who is made a living aid to souls and the holy possession of the children of God. And with Jesus the Spirit of Jesus, who is the Holy Spirit, who proceeds from the Father and the Son. This communication of divine life, this life which is called supernatural because it exceeds the capacity and native aptitude of every creature, is the eternal life of the Father, communicated eternally by the generation of the Son and through the breathing forth of the Holy Spirit, transmitted in time through an inconceivable effusion of love to creatures capable of receiving it. Its effusion to these poor creatures and its social constitution through Jesus Christ is the Church.

This life, then, descends to the Church and proceeds from the heart of the Father through the Son, in the Holy Spirit. The society of the children of God is the created receptacle of the divine life, the divine organism of creatures given the life which was in the Father, who has mercifully desired to communicate it to these poor creatures through Jesus Christ crucified. The eternal indwelling of the Divine Persons is extended in the Church. It is the indwelling of God in His creatures supernaturally vivified, and the ineffable circulation of the infinite life in souls in grace. Every drop of supernatural life which falls on a soul, like a dewdrop on a petal, comes from those eternal springs of living water emanating from the heavenly Father. The rich current of graces which irrigates the Church in heaven, in purgatory, and on earth flows from that inexhaustible source which eternally gives life to the Son and the Holy Spirit. The first and profound beginning of the Church is in the Father, and from the Father the Church proceeds by the merciful generation of free and

---

2 John 3:16.

generous love. We cannot go back any further. Here we reach the sacred heights of being and of life as we arrive at the beginning of all things. From this deep and fruitful abyss of life comes the life of the Church. When, on the wings of faith, we reach the sources of the great gift of the supernatural life, we cannot tarry elsewhere. We find the vivifying Spirit, the soul of a soul in grace, the vital and infinite principle of the Church, the source of her gifts, the root of her charisms. Yet the Spirit proceeds from the Father through the Son, as was remarked by the Greek Fathers,[3] and it is necessary to go higher, if not as regards being, then as regards origin. We then arrive at the Son, from whose sacrifice the Holy Spirit comes to us. But the Son receives everything equally from the Father. The Son made man continually turns with love to the Father, to whom He refers everything and whose sovereign will is the secret and pleasing food with which the Son nurtures Himself.[4] It is necessary to ascend still higher because it is impossible to stop with the Son. We reach the Father, who receives life from no one. Here is the sacred source which animates and sanctifies the Church. Is it strange, then, that the return movement of the Church to its beginning is directed to and seeks the Father through Jesus Christ?

Since the Church is animated by the Holy Spirit, who comes to her as the soul of the fullness of Jesus, she must necessarily return to Jesus as she is moved, impelled, and inspired by the Holy Spirit toward Him. Here we find the roots of this fervent, indefatigable, and heroic love of the Church for Jesus. It originates in this same soul of life and fire. Yet, in finding Jesus and in embracing Him, in making herself one in spirit with her Bridegroom, necessarily with her Bridegroom,

---

[3] Cf. Amor Rimbal, *Fundamental Problems,* chapter v, "The Exposition of the Catholic Theory of the Greek Fathers concerning the Trinity."
[4] Cf. John 4:32.

in the unity of the Spirit of Love which embraces them both, the Church must fly to the Father, to whom all the affections and thoughts of the soul of Jesus go. The Church thus continually ascends to this adorable source of life: "Per Dominum nostrum Jesum Christum Filium tuum," as she repeats each hour in her prayers — "Through Jesus Christ our Lord, Thy Son." This is how the Church prays, loves, and lives. Her life is a continual aspiration breathed forth to the heavenly Father, a constantly renewed ascent to the sacred source of life, an unceasing movement of love towards Him who loved her so much that He gave her His Son and in giving Him gave all. An infant does not seek the breast of its mother more impetuously than the Church seeks the fruitful bosom of the heavenly Father. The child in formation within the body of its mother is not more closely united to the mother's life than the Church to that of the eternal Father. We have nothing in this world adequate for portraying the vital and intimate love of the Church for the Father, the mysterious vivifying union and dependence of the Spouse of Jesus on the Father of Jesus, who is also the Father of the Church and of souls.

All the holy relationships we have studied thus far hinge on this fundamental one. The saints, the angels, the Blessed Virgin, Jesus, the Holy Spirit, intimately united as the life of the Church — all these have their origin in this eminent reality of the life of the Father, which eternally and without diminution goes to the Son and the Holy Spirit and, in time and in due proportion, to creatures sanctified by the touch of grace. Just as in the intellect in action there live and subsist, though fleetingly, thoughts which spring forth in our minds, so in this eternal communication of the life of the Father to the Son and to the Holy Spirit all the relations which the supernatural life places in the Church reside and have their basis. And in this communication, the being and life of the Holy

Spouse of Jesus Christ have their root. The love of the Church could have no other source. That which has its first principle in the Father must return to Him through an ordered return of love. Jesus found power and repose in the love of the Father and in His adorable will: the Church finds her vigor and joy in the sovereign will of the Father. The heart of the Spouse of Jesus, incited and made into a burning coal of love by the Spirit of Jesus, cannot rest in time or in eternity, except in the heart of the heavenly Father.

III

With this explanation we have attained the sacred heights towards which love impels the Church and the divine source of life. Beyond this we cannot go. The life and the action of the Church will have reached fullness of vigor when, having fulfilled her purposes in the world, the Spouse of Jesus Christ will take her repose and be joyfully submerged in the immense sea of the life of the heavenly Father. At that time God will have completed His sublime plan for the Church and the whole of creation. Then the living being of the Church will be displayed before the divine countenance, in numberless delights, in the light of glory which never ends. For this purpose God made the universe and placed the Church in its midst. All creatures together, transformed in the light of natural understanding and in the flame of love placed in God and praising the one from whom they receive these, would be but a small thing in the face of supernatural understanding, love, and praise of the Church. God has desired to give Himself this tribute of omnipotent love shown in sanctified creation. He has desired that this living praise of His being and His perfections should be as divine as the being to whom it was directed. This praise is the Church, now seen in the shadows of the faith and amid the trials of life, but later to be seen in the light of glory and the raptures of beatific love. When the Church has completed her task; that is, when all those souls who have not steadfastly resisted love have been gained for Christ, when all the members of the Church have been rid of their earthly cares, when these bodies which are now the temple of the Holy Spirit through grace are rapt in glory, and when the Church is displayed in her full glory, her whole being and its every living part will be the living, immortal, and divine praise of the august Trinity.

Since the Church has been created for such a high and glorious destiny, it is necessary that the whole of creation should be subject to her and be disposed to do her bidding. All is for the Church, as the Church is for Jesus and Jesus for God.[5] Everything is complete in the Church or attains its consummation in her, as the Church does in Jesus. Outside the divine order there is only dislocation in being and error in the evaluation of things. Peoples and nations, heaven and earth, are all intended for the Church, as the pedestal is intended for the statue placed on it which is resplendent with the majesty of art. Everything in the universe must serve the purpose of the Church and everything in the human order must submit to the infallible law of her doctrine. No matter what the ends, powers, and achievements of creatures may be, they shall not enter into order nor be fruitful in what Providence has destined them for, if they do not subject themselves to the divine plan, at whose center is Jesus Christ extended in His Church, in which alone they receive the holy assignment which links them hierarchically with God. The world and mankind are meant for the Church, in order that the Church may sanctify and supernaturally elevate them as they become incorporated in her divine being. They exist and

---

5Cf. I Cor. 3:22-23.

subsist for the formation of the Church. When the last hour has come, God will consider ended His work of many centuries and He will have put the final touch of life in the Church. Then the heavens will fold back like an immense curtain, the elements of the world will fuse into a new heaven and earth, and man's empires and powers shall pass forever like a dream dispelled by a ray of daylight. Everything in this world will have passed. In eternity the Church will gloriously live in God. The damned and the rebellious angels will then be accursed and powerless dross in hell, a stupendous declaration of the triumph of the holy Spouse of the Lamb who with the Father and the Holy Spirit lives and reigns forever.

CONCLUSION

We have come to the end of our long journey. In our book THE CATHOLIC CHURCH: THE MYSTICAL BODY OF CHRIST, we considered the reality of the Church, unparalleled in the world, and we examined the marvels of organization, of life, of holy activity found in it. We have now treated the Church's eminent position in the universal order of things, and we have studied the relationships it has with everything on earth and in heaven.

In this holy organism we live our life as children of God. Outside it this life is not possible, and only when wholly within the Church can we in an orderly way reach the maturity and fullness of the supernatural life. We receive it from the Church, and in the Church it grows, prospers, and reaches its culmination at the proper time.

Man intimately loves the family into which he was born and, within the family the father and mother whose blood and name he possesses. He loves the country in which he lives and in which he was educated. He loves its skies, its fields, its mountains, its customs, its history, all of which he holds in the depths of his heart. He loves the country under whose protection his people live, the country whose glory he considers his own, in whose traditions, culture, language, and social environment his mind has been cultivated, and whose social, glorious and fruitful life he comes to love more than his very own, so that at a solemn crisis he is willing to offer his blood for this, his earthly mother. All these loves are born of nature and are firmly rooted in the heart. They are the spontaneous movement of man vigorously adhering to the solid stock whence he comes, a stock whose roots have deeply penetrated the fertile field of the natural institutions necessary for life.

The Christian has his mother, his family, and his spiritual country in the Church. Everything supernatural he receives from her, and only in her can he keep and develop it. God has planted in the Christian heart a profound love of the Church, a delicate and sensitive love in which are present all the desires of all holy loves which dwell in the heart, but elevated to the divine order.

For him who strives to live the Christian life fully, the Church is an imperious necessity; and love for her is the noble soaring of a soul rising to God as it seeks Him in the holy unity of the Mystical Body.

To spurn the Church is a tremendous misfortune for a man, a monstrous aberration in a Christian.

To love the Church is a sacred duty of the children of God who are born of her and in her grow and reach the sanctified fullness of glory. The Church is mother and family, home and country for souls in the life which unites them with Jesus Christ. To love the Church is a requirement of good order. To spurn her and, worse, to hate her, is the horrible sin of a base and miserable son.

To live in the Church is to approach the holy ark outside which there is no salvation.

To live the life of the Church is to possess the life of God within ourselves and to form ourselves for heaven, to which the Church surely brings us.

To die in the holy bosom of the Church, illumined by her faith, sustained by her hope and animated by her charity, is to close our eyes to the trials of the present life and to open them to the glorious light of eternity in the holy arms of the mother who will never leave us.

Nineteen centuries have passed since Jesus gave us the gift of His Church. Only Jesus could tell of the stream of goods which this holy Mother of the children of God has given to the world. Only He could tell of the innumerable souls she has snatched from the power of Satan and of the many souls who now give honor and glory in heaven to the source of all things. The centuries which remain will be no less fruitful. The Church, as Jesus does, purifies and cleanses what she touches, and her journey throughout the world is, like that of the Saviour, a great and flourishing source of benefits. The drops of her blood are fruitful. As they come down upon earth, they give to it souls who live for God in Jesus Christ. The Church is the continuation of Jesus Christ among men. Through the Church, Christ lives among the sons of Adam and does good wherever she is allowed to remain. The Church is the glorious arc of light through which souls enkindled with charity pass over the threshold of death, leaving this valley of tears for the active and glorious participation in the vision of God.